WORLD OF
THE MAKERS

WORLD OF THE MAKERS

Today's Master Craftsmen and Craftswomen

Text and Photography by Edward Lucie-Smith

PADDINGTON PRESS LTD

THE TWO CONTINENTS
PUBLISHING GROUP

Library of Congress Cataloging in Publication Data

Lucie-Smith, Edward.
    World of the makers.

    1. Handicraft.   2. Artisans.   I. Title.
TT149.L82   1975   745.5'092'2 [B]   74-15916

ISBN 0-8467-0037-9
LC 74-15916

© Copyright 1975 Paddington Press Ltd
Printed in the U.S.A.

Computer typeset by Input Typesetting Ltd.,
4 Valentine Place, London S.E.1, England

Design by Richard Browner

IN THE UNITED STATES
PADDINGTON PRESS LTD
TWO CONTINENTS PUBLISHING GROUP
30 East 42 Street
New York City, N.Y. 10017
U.S.A.

IN THE UNITED KINGDOM
PADDINGTON PRESS LTD
1 Wardour Street
London W1
England

IN CANADA
distributed by
RANDOM HOUSE OF CANADA LTD
370 Alliance Avenue
Toronto, Ontario
M6N 2H8

Contents

1
2
3
4
5
6
7
8
9
10

This book is a fan letter – but a fan letter for adults. Despite the ever-increasing activity which has been taken in the crafts over a number of years – an interest which has manifested itself in the publication of numerous books, and in the rising number of people who feel the ambition to become craftsmen – I feel an important area of contemporary creativity is being neglected and misunderstood. Almost the most useful form of admiration is criticism. Good criticism cannot exist unless the foundations have been soundly laid. I would like to cut back some of the undergrowth and allow the true shape of craft activity to reveal itself.

An objection might be raised here that the crafts *are* appreciated, that the Crafts Revival is already with us. My answer to this objection is a qualified "yes."

It *is* already with us, but we have not understood its significance, either in relation to the society we inhabit, or in relation to the artistic activity which that society generates. My aim here, in addition to trying to show some of the range and quality of what is being done, is to allow leading craftsmen to speak for themselves, and to put one point of view beside another until something like a total picture emerges.

What I want to do is to look at the crafts in aesthetic terms, and also in human terms. What do these activities signify within their own discipline? What is the significance of the contribution they make to society as a whole? More important even than this – what kinds of people are involved with the crafts, and what are their reasons for doing what they do?

Anyone who studies the literature of the modern crafts soon becomes aware that it is rich in books of three kinds. First and rarest (though perhaps the most influential) are the books which are "inspirational" in character. Much that the famous potter Bernard Leach has written falls into this category. Second, and more numerous, are the "how to" books – handbooks on making pottery, on weaving techniques, on metalwork and on jewelry. Finally, there are books which illustrate the work of leading contemporary craftsmen – usually these have brief biographical statements or a technical commentary attached to the illustrations, or sometimes both together. Books in this last category seem designed to serve either as catalogues to exhibitions, or as guides for collectors of the crafts. What is lacking is a book which speaks of the craftsman as hero, as Vasari in his *Lives* spoke of the painters and sculptors who made the Renaissance.

It is not my intention to follow Vasari's method, which is at once too ambitious and too rigid for my purpose. But biographical material seems to me a legitimate part of my scheme. Still more so are the opinions held by the craftsmen themselves. The foundation of my edifice is therefore a series of interviews with men and women whose work I admire. It is their thoughts which have guided me in writing what follows, even though there are one or two cases where the subject of the interview has preferred to not be quoted directly. These interviews took place in the craftsmen's own environments, in the places where they live and work. The photographs which accompany the text are designed to illuminate what was said, not only by illustrating a number of craft processes, but by saying more about the atmosphere in which they took place than words alone can do. Our long conversations – some occupied the best part of a day – had no formality about them. They took place as the work process proceeded; and many of the questions and answers arose directly from what I saw taking place. Perhaps the most valuable of all were answers to questions which had remained unspoken – spontaneous observations prompted by the activity itself.

Yet there are also certain frontiers to define. Enthusiasm for the crafts has led to a very loose definition of the area they may be supposed to cover. This is a book about the sophisticated craftsman, who is as keenly conscious of his own role as the so-called fine artist. Of deliberate choice, there is nothing about the "traditional" or "country" crafts. I put these descriptive words into quotation marks because they have long served to perpetuate sentimental misunderstandings about craft activity. It is true that the vigorous craft scene of today has its roots in a reaction against the industrialism of the nineteenth century. But the reaction contained the seeds of misunderstanding. Like many revolutions, it felt the need to disguise itself as a return to tradition. But this alone was not the root of the trouble.

In all societies, people feel the need to preserve the past: they seek to encapsulate and keep unaltered those areas of the past which seem to have aesthetic or symbolic value. The great museums – the British Museum, the Louvre, the Metropolitan Museum in New York – are in essence mechanisms for doing this. But the impulse extends a long way beyond the boundaries of the museum building and museum activity. In England, for example, there has been the continuous struggle, in the middle and latter part of this century, to preserve the beautiful anachronism of the country house. Everyone knows that great mansions are now economic and social nonsense. But most people feel that their loss would leave society immeasurably poorer. Thus, the effort has been made to preserve them and to provide a kind of justification for their existence. The effort has led to many paradoxes, some injustices, and a few tragedies. We have seen stately homes turned into fun-fairs and council offices. Where grants are concerned, the principle has sometimes seemed to be "unto him that hath, much shall be given." On the other hand, a few people have lived wretchedly in order to preserve a building they loved and considered important. We have gradually come to realize that what the country mansion needs, wherever possible, is the warmth of human presence and human activity, because these explain why it was conceived in the first place and how both architect and patron expected it to function. Even if well preserved, a country house without an occupant is like the snailshell without the snail, dead and hollow. Yet we are often at a loss to devise mechanisms which will enable the families who now own these houses to continue to live in them, without on the one hand assuming too heavy a financial burden, or, upon the other, being exempted from the burdens which weigh on the rest of us.

The analogy between the need to preserve the great country houses and the need to preserve the traditional crafts has, however, only a limited application.

When we speak of the traditional crafts, we are doing more than discuss a series of quaint survivals, and we are also speaking of activities which are not necessarily confined to the countryside. The term can legitimately be applied to the manufacturer of corn dollies; we can also affix it to the work of the top-class tailor or the maker of hand-lasted boots. It is surprising how many skills of this type survive on the margins of our complex industrial society; and they survive, for the most part, because there is still a demand for them. The gunsmiths and the saddlers have full order books, and what they make has a technical proficiency which surpasses the work of their predecessors. The modern racing saddle, for instance, has a refinement which makes its eighteenth-century equivalent look terribly clumsy and unsuited to its purpose.

When a skill is preserved after the need for it has gone, then it turns into an exercise in pure virtuosity. It is the knowing how to do it, and not the end product, which gives delight. If enthusiasts strive to preserve certain peasant skills,

why should we try to deny them their pleasure? Yet it must be recognized that crafts exercised in this way, for their own sake, or in simple rejection of the modern world and its assumed evils, seldom produce objects which are particularly interesting to look at. The object becomes a certificate that the chosen process has been followed through to the end. Aesthetic response has nothing to do with it.

By contrast, aesthetic response has everything to do with the activity of the craftsmen who are the subject of this book. It is true that their products can be used, but the degree of practicability varies a great deal according to the craft they practice and the situation in which they find themselves. Three of the potters whose work is discussed here either themselves produce, or oversee the production, of a range of kitchenware. All three would be desolated if the casseroles they make did not serve, and serve well, the purpose for which they are designed. On the other hand, one of the bookbinders remarked to me that a book, by the time he had done with it, was to be regarded primarily as an art object, and no longer as something to be read. He told me "the only bookbinder's joke I know," about a client who brings a book to the binder who has just created an elaborate and beautiful livery for it. "Look at this," he says. "I've only just got it from you, and the damn thing is falling to pieces!" The bookbinder takes the offending item and scrutinizes it carefully. "Ah," he replies. "I'm afraid you've opened it."

This joke facetiously illustrates one extreme in the disregard for utility. Facetiousness aside, however, the desire to give delight prevails among a majority of contemporary craftsmen. The craftsman is as self-aware as the so-called fine artist. He has as much right to speak, and as much to say for himself, as the painter or sculptor. Like the painter and the sculptor, he is the product of the complex society wherein we all live, and this is true whether he resides in a large town or in the heart of the country.

In addition to avoiding the subject of the country crafts, I have also made the decision to avoid any discussion of the ethnic craft products which are now to be found in specialist stores in large cities throughout both the United States and Western Europe. These craft products find a ready market for a variety of reasons. They are cheap, colorful and carry with them a hint of the exotic. Their textures and materials make a pleasing contrast with the manufactured objects we use for most jobs in our homes. Since they are handmade, they humanize our interiors and enable us to add our own touch of individual fantasy.

Yet these objects are also the skeletons at the feast. As I look into the shop windows which display them, I see them as emblems of the injustices of western society and of the way western culture poisons the other cultures with which it comes in contact. And this is true even when the shops have behind them (as they so often do) a charitable purpose. I cannot help feeling that the people who make these things come to us as beggars, and that this is degrading to them and still more so to us. The low prices often go hand-in-hand with the shoddy quality of the craft itself. If one knows anything about the work produced in the past in the "underdeveloped" countries which supply these outlets, one notices that the work being done in the present, directed as it is toward a market which understands little about the original purpose of some of the objects, and less about the symbolism which is often part of their fabric, is a sadly degenerate version of what used to be made, carried out hurriedly, in poor materials, blurred copies of originals which had splendid vigor.

The western craftsmen whom I describe here exist not only upon the same footing, but in precisely the same context as the rest of us. They are subject to the same influences, read the same newspapers, go to the same plays, watch the same films and television shows. As sensitive and creative people, their thinking is often in advance of that of society taken as a whole. Indeed, as I hope to prove, their supposed traditionalism has served to disguise the fact that they are a new and original element in the world we inhabit, with an importance quite out of proportion to their numbers.

Their existence raises one or two questions which it is worth stating immediately. The first is that of the apparent isolation of the craft scene. Those who call themselves artists and those who call themselves craftsmen seldom exhibit together. Official support comes to artists and craftsmen through different channels. They have carefully separate professional organizations. Art critics seldom write about the crafts, and such professional criticism of the crafts as there is tends to be purely technical in its approach. It may seem an odd comparison, but I am reminded of the relationship which till recently existed between science fiction and the rest of modern literature.

Science fiction can be looked at in two ways. One can see it, primarily, as an offshoot of mass culture — in this resembling jazz, which has its roots in popular music, but which appeals, in fact, to a minority public. Like the jazz public, the science fiction public has, or had, a keen sense of its own identity. If one considers the readership of science fiction, one notices a number of things which tend to set it apart. There are science fiction congresses, and the so-called fanzines — periodicals which address themselves to hobbyists who take an obsessional interest in the genre. Until a few years ago, all discussion of the merits or demerits of a particular piece of science fiction writing was conducted within the closed world which SF itself provided. SF writers were as happy to be ignored by professional critics of literature as those critics were to pass them by.

This situation changed when a few people began to look at science fiction from a different angle. They recognized that, for all its pop trappings, it was the place where the epic had contrived to re-root itself. They recognized, too, that it could accommodate the fable and the allegory. As the tradition of the realistic novel broke up, earlier fictional forms began to surface again; and SF was the beneficiary. But critics were slow to realize that some of the most admired creators of contemporary prose narrative — William Golding and Herman Hesse among them — often ventured into territory which was best described as science fictional. Or, rather, the SF label seemed to demean the literary quality of what the writers produced. So for a long time the genre was deprived of some of its brightest talents. People refused to see their close connection with a great mass of perhaps inferior writing which nevertheless pursued the same aims, and adopted much the same strategies in order to do so. It was only with the advent of a generation of writers such as J. G. Ballard and Brian Aldiss, which had actually cut its teeth in the science fiction magazines, and which had published its first full-length works under the science fiction label, that finally persuaded professional critics to take the genre seriously.

The work of the artist-craftsman seems to have suffered the rather similar fate of being pushed into a special ghetto of its own. Where an effort is made to outline the standards by which it ought to be judged, these standards are always referred back to the grammar of the particular activity. There is no attempt to construct an aesthetic that might embrace both contemporary painting and sculpture and the contemporary crafts. Instead, judgments are limited by two unstated and self-contradictory assumptions. The first is rooted in the early history of the craft revival — the time when it was chiefly thought of as a passionate revolt against industrialism and its consequences. It is that the craftsman must always exist in opposition to the modern; and that his only connection with modern art is therefore to act as a critic of its excesses, both through what he is and what he produces. The second assumption is that the craftsman can only become modern by adapting ideas which the fine artist has already invented; and that his success must be judged by the skill with which he performs this act of translation.

Neither of these assumptions has much to recommend it; and one can, as it happens, pursue two rather different lines of argument, both of which lead toward precisely the same conclusion. The one is based on an examination of our attitudes toward the achievements of the past, and especially of the way in which we present these achievements in our great museums. The thoughtful museum visitor soon begins to notice that the division between the fine arts and what are sometimes called the decorative arts has never been entirely immutable; and that it is, in any case, not only a thing of recent growth, but a special feature of western art as opposed to the art produced by other cultures. When we look at the legacy bequeathed to us by the civilizations of the ancient world, we discover that some of the objects which we are readiest to call masterpieces are things which today would be described as craftwork rather than artwork. They include the Portland Vase in the British Museum, the archaic Chinese bronzes in Peking, London and Stockholm, and most of Tutankhamen's treasure in the Cairo Museum.

Similarly, when we examine the history of a style, such as Mannerism, we see that it cannot be judged on painting and sculpture alone, but that all the artifacts produced under its influence must be brought into consideration, if we are to gain a true idea of its potential as a force for change.

My other argument is based on what we can see happening in modern art. Essentially, what has taken place in the visual arts in the years since the Second World War is a gradual breakdown of categories. It might seem that this breakdown meant simply the abolition of the barrier which once divided painting and sculpture, so that what the spectator had to deal with was an art object, whether in three dimensions or in two. On a second look, one is aware that the breakdown of categories extends much further than this. The visual arts are no longer purely visual – the artist ventures into any field that suits him. He makes use of sound and movement. Time becomes almost as important an element in his language as the modulation of color and surface. His work is often "environmental" – that is, it acts as a kind of surrogate for architecture. He raids the physical sciences and philosophy.

Though the visual artist now makes claims to be a kind of universal man, reviving the Renaissance concept in a new and less convincing guise, he is less receptive to what he considers raids upon his own territory from other disciplines. He is unwilling to admit, for instance, that those who call themselves artist-craftsmen are often working along precisely the same lines as himself, and doing so with a greater degree of skill and sophistication. The modernist, when he condescends to make objects, sees himself, not as a man who makes a representation of things found in nature, but as one who adds to nature inventions which she herself has not thought of — new forms, new relationships of color. The test of what he makes is that it should compete successfully with the natural order, in the degree of spiritual and intellectual involvement which it produces in the man who looks at it. The craftsman may not have quite so ambitious an aim, but his purpose has always been to produce forms, colors and textures which are, as he says "convincing." That is, they must have sufficient integrity and individuality to satisfy the eye, no matter in what surroundings they are placed.

One minor by-product of the interest now being taken by fine artists in what they dub "object quality" has been a series of experiments with forms and techniques. There is now no agreed method of making a picture, even among artists who are still content, with no further qualification, to be described as painters. It is no longer a matter of putting paint on canvas. The surface is colored by means of a controlled staining process, so that support and surface in fact become one. The canvas may be cut and the strips re-woven. Occasionally the painting is adorned with beads and plaited strings. Three-dimensional objects are sewn, and then stuffed. Sculptures are made of all kinds of materials, ranging from steel mesh and sections of I-beams to ceramic material and rope.

All of this makes the distinction between the arts and the crafts as difficult to maintain as the barriers between the various categories in the fine arts. Let us take a hypothetical example which, as we shall see later, may not remain hypothetical for long. There are two creators. One is a man with a background in the fine arts. He has, shall we say, won acceptance as a sculptor. He decides that his next sculpture will be a book (the artist R. B. Kitaj has, after all, made a series of prints which are literal presentations of the covers or dust jackets of favorite books). If he wanted simply to imitate a book, he could cast it in a material such as sculpmetal. But since he actually wants to make one, he teaches himself the processes of bookbinding. In his next exhibition of sculpture the book duly appears. I would be very surprised if anyone challenged its right to be there, or the maker's right to describe it simply as sculpture.

But what would happen if a well-known bookbinder were to say, in however mild a voice, that he regarded one of his products as sculptural, and wished it to be judged on the same level as contemporary sculpture? However brilliant his skills, he would run the risk of being described as pretentious. And this in spite of the fact that his work, in a technical sense, would almost certainly be superior to that of the sculptor described above.

The question which arises here is whether there is any longer much point in maintaining a division between the fine arts and the crafts; and whether, indeed, the term artist-craftsman is not a tautology. The problem is complex, and I am in no haste to solve it here, though I believe that we shall arrive at some tentative answers in the course of this book.

One point, however, seems to me worth raising immediately, because it puts the question itself into a different perspective. This is the status of the craftsman in a society very different from our own — that of Japan. The Japanese crafts have long been a matter of particular fascination to the artist-craftsmen who have worked in the west, and particularly to the potters. The fruitful relationship between Bernard Leach and Shoji Hamada had immensely important consequences for the development of twentieth-century ceramics. But Leach saw in the Japanese attitude to ceramics a model for a return to the source, one might even say for a return to nature.

What strikes me, on the other hand, is the lack of established hierarchies among the various forms of artistic expression which are practiced in Japan. I am also struck by the way in which the craftsman is valued by contemporary Japanese as the symbol of the best their society can produce, to the point where certain individuals are officially designated as Living Cultural Treasures. The term may seem to us quaint, but the attitude of mind which it embodies is surely something we ought to find admirable.

As far as I can discover, Japan, despite the existence of Shintoism and of different varieties of Buddhism, among them the now (with westerners) immensely fashionable Zen, has long possessed a society which is predominantly secular in tone. The work of art took the place of objects whose meaning was more specifically religious; and when we look at Japanese writings about art we see that the art-object is thought of as possessing an indefinable but nevertheless very powerful numinousness. The tea-ceremony, and the values attached to tea-ceremony objects are a striking instance of the way feelings which we in the west would call religious, and others which we would describe as aesthetic, intermingle to the point where they cannot usefully be separated.

In the western democracies, during the years since the Second World War, there has been an increasing tendency for the museum to replace the cathedral as the shrine of values that go beyond the materialistic standards which apply to everyday life. As belief in the supernatural dwindled almost to vanishing, belief in the semi-divine power of artistic talent grew correspondingly. The heroization of Picasso, and of a handful of other artists connected with the Modern Movement, can of course be paralleled by the honors which were paid both publicly and privately to Michelangelo during his own lifetime. But Michelangelo is an exceptional case. Now we are ready to pay tribute to almost all comers, provided they claim to possess of the creative spark.

In part, this attitude can be connected with secularism itself. In worshipping the artist, we burn incense at the altar we have raised to human perfectibility, or at least to the notion that man's potential is limitless. At the same time, as Freud was probably the first to point out in his brilliant

Civilization and its Discontents, art and religion can serve interchangeably as palliatives for the restraints which civilization imposes upon us.

All this granted, why do we go on preserving a hierarchical structure in the visual arts? Such a structure cuts clean across our insistence, not only on the boundlessness of man's talents, but on the need to reject anything that might prevent them from fulfilling their potential. A number of answers suggest themselves – though none, I think, is completely convincing.

One, the most obvious, is the power of convention. Since the division between the fine arts and the applied arts has existed for so long, we accept it as immutable. Again, there is the mistrust of virtuosity which has increasingly marked our attitude toward painting and sculpture.

We assume that an insistence upon technical prowess means that the work lacks original content. We are interested in the marks left by the artist's struggle with his conception because they seem to guarantee that the embodiment we see before us is the product of original thought. The craftsman's pride in his own skill, and the finesse with which he employs it, often seem to us the things which serve to divide the craftwork from the artwork. Japanese potters have evolved an interesting riposte to this attitude by evolving a kind of virtuosity which results in apparent roughness – not an art that conceals art but a skill that disguises skill. Finally, we tend to feel that the work of the artist-craftsman

lacks scale, that his statement is essentially private. One can counter this by pointing out that most modern paintings and sculptures are also private statements, though the scale may range from the minuscule to the gigantic. And if we admit things like tapestry and stained glass into the circle of the crafts, then lack of scale is not necessarily a craft characteristic. Here, as elsewhere, definitions tend to be governed by our subjective attitude, as much as by what we know objectively.

Some readers may ask why I have, in this case, elected to confine my researches chiefly to a relatively small group of craftsmen living and working in England. There are in fact several reasons for this restriction.

In the first place, England is the place where the craft revival has a continuous history since its inception in the mid-nineteenth century. In the second place, though England is a small country, it is sufficiently various, both geographically and socially, to offer a wide variety of situations to the craftsman. He can elect to live in the heart of the country, or in the metropolis; he can exist in close contact with the community that surrounds him, or almost completely cut off from it. I have tried to explore a wide variety of personal situations in this book, just as I have tried to span the generations. In addition, I have deliberately chosen to interview people who came from a wide variety of social backgrounds, and who arrived at their vocation as craftsmen in very different ways.

Though a number of my subjects are Americans

now living and working in Britain, it is necessary, I think, to point out one or two respects in which the American craft scene (in most respects broadly similar to the British one) differs from its counterpart on this side of the Atlantic. The differences which seem to me most striking are as follows: first, Americans excel in certain skills which are not so highly developed over here. There are, for instance, more good glassmakers in America; and American enamelers have achieved a virtuosity much in advance of ours. In furniture making, as we shall see, there is a well-defined difference in taste. British craftsmen do not make the carved "free form" furniture, halfway to being true sculpture, which is an American specialty. Similarly, British work in plastics tends to be a good deal less ambitious — perhaps because British contemporary sculptors have tended to monopolize the use of plastics on a large scale.

There are, in addition, some differences of taste, and in the pattern of education. The idea of "funk," which for some time dominated the thinking of younger American craftsmen, especially ceramists, and more especially those who live and work on the West Coast, has made little progress in England, and does not seem likely to do so.

Finally, there is a difference in the way that craftsmen are trained, (although this is less fundamental than it looks at first). Lee Nordness, in his introduction to *Objects USA* – a book which, for all its inadequacies, is still one of the most comprehensive surveys of the American crafts –

points out that many younger craftsmen have a university background. In fact, not merely their education but their actual training in the crafts they practice took place under university auspices.

In Britain, art schools have until recently remained separate from the universities. Despite the recent incorporation of many of them into the structure of regional polytechnics, they continue to have a separate identity. Yet, looked at from another angle, the British system of education, in a smaller and more centralized country, is also as a whole correspondingly closer knit. America seems to have no equivalent of the Royal College of Art in London, a partly post-graduate institution which brings together particularly promising artists, designers and craftsmen. As we shall see, it has exercised a powerful influence on the careers of some of the younger craftsmen who I interviewed.

What counts, however is that these, like their American contemporaries, are people who are, in the non-pejorative sense, middle-class. Their lives are shaped, not by the fact that they have inherited a particular vocation, a trade handed down from father to son, but by their own deliberate choice. This choice is governed by ability and by temperament, but very often it implies a criticism of the kind of society we live in. Such a broadly-defined criticism is, in part, the heritage of the immediate historical antecedents of the contemporary crafts scene. In my next chapter I will attempt briefly to sketch the historical background of the crafts movement as we now know it.

The twentieth-century artist-craftsman is best thought of as the heir and direct descendant of the Arts and Crafts Movement. This movement flourished during the latter part of the nineteenth century and continued its activities in the years immediately preceding the First World War. The origins of both the contemporary craftsman and of the Arts and Crafts Movement can, however, be traced to a much earlier period.

England was the first country in the world to feel the impact of the Industrial Revolution, and she was also the first to show signs of a reaction against it. Blake's denunciation of the "dark satanic mills" was followed in 1829 by Thomas Carlyle's sorrowful observation that "On every hand the living artisan is driven from his workshop, to make room for a speedier inanimate one. The shuttle drops from the fingers of the weaver, and falls into iron fingers that play it faster." Meanwhile, on a practical level, the Luddites of 1811 were succeeded by the machine-wreckers of the 1830's.

Perhaps the first designer to look for a practical alternative to what industry seemed determined to impose upon society and the environment was Augustus Welby Pugin. Pugin was the most talented exponent of the second, more scholarly phase of the Gothic Revival; it is to him that we owe the astonishing gothic decoration of the Houses of Parliament. Pugin's ideas were derived, at least in part, from his conversion to a fervent Roman Catholicism. He believed that the Reformation lay at the roots of the evils he saw around him, and he looked back with nostalgia to a "Merry England" where "the architecture was in keeping with the faith and manners of the time — at once strong and hospitable."

But Pugin also saw and denounced the impropriety of using gothic ornament, or gothic architectural features, for purposes for which they were never intended. He remarked drily that "A man who remains any length of time in a modern Gothic room and escapes without being wounded by some of its minutiae may consider himself fortunate."

Yet Pugin differed from the designers and theorists who were to come after him in seeing no harm in the use of machine processing. A "Christian architect" such as himself should know how to put the power of the machine to its proper use.

The next stage of the reaction against industrialism was initiated by John Ruskin. He had established his reputation in 1843 with the publication of the first volume of *Modern Painters*. In 1851 he brought out the first part of *The Stones of Venice,* which was destined to be his most influential work. Two further volumes followed in 1853, and there were to be numerous reprints during the next sixty years. The appearance of the first part of *The Stones of Venice* coincided with the Great Exhibition of 1851. Despite the general success of the venture, and the huge throngs of visitors attracted by it, intelligent critics had been dismayed by an almost universal lack of taste in manufactured articles, and there were calls (for example in *The Times*), for something to be done about it. Ruskin wanted more than a mere reform of the way things looked; he also wanted a radical reconsideration of the way in which they were made.

The most influential part of Ruskin's argument was a defense of the hand-made against the machine-made, because the former reflects man's own essential humanity. "Men," said Ruskin, "were not intended to work with the accuracy of tools, to be precise and perfect in all their actions. If you would have that precision out of them, and make their fingers measure degrees like cogwheels, and their arms strike curves like compasses, you must unhumanise them." Later he was to propound the rule that one must "never demand an exact finish for its own sake, but only for some practical or noble end."

Among those most impressed by Ruskin's arguments were the young men who were to form the Pre-Raphaelite Brotherhood. The second part of *The Stones of Venice,* which contains the famous chapter "On the Nature of Gothic" was published during William Morris's first year as an undergraduate at Oxford. The book helped to confirm him in his vocation, which was to do something in the arts. At first, however, Morris was not sure what this was to be. He discovered that he was not destined to be either a painter or an architect.

It was the experience of building, decorating and furnishing the Red House (his first married home) in 1860 which led Morris to see that there was something both useful and urgent to be done in the realm of design. The creation of the Red House led, in turn, to the setting up of the Firm, a venture in which most of the Pre-Raphaelites were to cooperate. At first on an informal basis, and later more professionally, the artists connected with the Brotherhood began to apply their talents to the decorative arts. From furnishing their own homes, they moved on to a general interest in decoration.

Ford Madox Brown, a painter who was somewhat senior to the rest, and who was never officially a Pre-Raphaelite Brother, was, in the beginning, the only one with any practical experience as a designer. His bold, simple furniture was to be immensely influential in the Arts and Crafts Movement as a whole. Pieces recognizably related to it were being made by Gustav Stickley's Craftsman Workshops, in Syracuse, New York, and even by purely commercial firms in Grand Rapids, Michigan, during the early years of the present century. But it was Morris himself who was to guide the fortunes of the new venture, and it was he who had sole charge of Morris and Co. after 1875.

By this time, its reputation was already long established. The vital first step came with the International Exhibition at South Kensington in 1862. The Firm's exhibits were awarded two gold medals, and the jury praised them for "the exactness of the imitation" of medieval detail. The reason that Morris and his associates were at first thought of as copyists rather than innovators was that they scored their earliest success with stained glass. There was a brisk demand for this, as numerous churches were being built to serve the needs of an expanding population. Morris understood, perhaps better than anyone since the middle ages, the principles upon which medieval stained glass had been designed, and contemporaries were bowled over by the strength and harmonious color of his and Burne-Jones's designs. Many of the firm's ecclesiastical commissions came from the architect G. T. Bodley, and such jobs were to supply a welcome source of income as long as the business lasted. But success in this field did tend to obscure the originality of thought which went into the Firm's other ventures.

Meanwhile, Morris began to discover his own genius as a designer of patterns for wallpapers and fabrics. This gift, like so many of his gifts, manifested itself slowly at first. He designed three wallpapers in 1864 but they were not commercially successful, and no more were created until 1871. Designs for textiles followed later still. Morris's first chintz dates from 1873, and he soon became so dissatisfied with the commercial printing and dyeing available to him that he embarked on a long series of investigations of traditional methods and dye-stuffs.

Morris papers and fabrics became very popular. It was a point of honor, among people who prided themselves on their good taste, to furnish their houses with nothing else. But Morris himself grew increasingly unhappy with a society in which only the relatively prosperous could afford his work. It is not too much to say that it was the commercial success of Morris and Company which led him along the path to socialism.

He had, of course, always recognized that the business catered for two different needs. First there was what he called "necessary workaday furniture," which must, he thought, be "simple to the last degree." Secondly there was "state-furniture." Inevitably, circumstances led him to concentrate on pieces in the latter category, because most of his commissions came from rich people who wanted to display their wealth, but his heart was really in the others. Despite this, some of the simplest Morris designs, notably the so-called Morris chair, and also some light rush-seated chairs based on traditional Sussex designs, were to become classics of their kind.

Morris was to come almost full circle in his attitudes to the machine: he at last came to recognize it, not merely as a necessary evil, but as a liberating force. In 1884 he spoke of "those miraculous machines, which if orderly forethought had dealt with them, might even now be speedily extinguishing all irksome and unintelligent labour."

His career is a crucial episode in the history of the crafts. He stands at the head of two quite different lines of development. One of these leads eventually to the designer-for-industry; more specifically, to the designer of domestic products. The men of the Bauhaus, and their Scandinavian successors, who between them revolutionized domestic taste in the twentieth century, owe a great deal to Morris because of his emphasis on the practical, and on the need to respect materials and to understand their characteristics and capacities. But the other line of descent leads to the artist-craftsmen of the present day, who often seem to be in revolt against the puritan simplicity and regularity which is the norm of modern industrial design.

Morris's successors were lesser men than he was, and they had a narrower vision. But it was their work which was to create the craft movement as we know it today. In particular, they put much greater emphasis than he did on the satisfaction which the craftsman himself derived from his labor; and on the work he did as being part of a better, because more integrated, way of life. These attitudes are still recognizable among contemporary craftsmen.

For the Arts and Crafts Movement, which provided a framework for the activities of the men of the second generation after Ruskin, the crucial decade was the 1880's. In 1882 Arthur Heygate Mackmurdo founded the Century Guild, in order, as he said, "to render all branches of art the sphere no longer of the tradesman, but of the artist." He planned to "restore building, decoration, glass painting, pottery, wood-carving and metal to their rightful place beside painting and sculpture." 1884 saw the foundation of the Art Workers' Guild, and in 1888 this in turn gave birth to the Arts and Crafts Exhibition Society. The title of this organisation is the first use of the term Arts and Crafts.

1888 was also the year in which Charles Robert Ashbee founded the Guild of Handicraft. The Guild sums up the achievement and the tragedy of the first phase of the craft revival, and exhibits some of its more conspicuously comic features as well. In particular, it demonstrates how precarious the revival was economically, and also the rigidity of social attitudes it still embodied.

Ashbee himself emerged from Toynbee Hall, the pioneer university settlement in the East End of London, and his attitudes remained those of an educator. But it was not only the public which was to receive instruction. Ashbee and those who worked with him were themselves self-taught, and great emphasis was placed on the learning process as the foundation of true style; "When a little group of men learn to pull together in a workshop, to trust each other, to play into each other's hands, and understand each other's limitations, their combination becomes creative, and the character they develop in themselves takes expression in the work of their fingers." Until 1895, a School of Handicraft was run in conjunction with the Guild.

At first Ashbee based himself in London. In 1890, he leased Essex House, which he described as "a stately Georgian mansion in Mile End." Since this was a long way from the fashionable quarters where he hoped his customers might be found, he also took showrooms in Mayfair.

In the first decade of its existence, Ashbee's enterprise enjoyed a considerable success, and became internationally famous. "Magpie and Stump," the house he built for himself in 1895 in Cheyne Walk, Chelsea, was illustrated and discussed as an example of Guild craftsmanship. In 1897, when Baillie Scott was commissioned to decorate the palace of the Grand Duke of Hesse at Darmstadt, it was the Guild that carried out the work. The guildsmen exhibited their products in Manchester, Liverpool, Dublin, Berlin, Munich, Frankfurt and Paris, and also as far afield as South Africa. The Guild itself, as an organisational model, provided the direct inspiration for Josef Hoffmann's Vienna Workshops.

A chance came in 1902, when the lease on Essex House ran out. Ashbee could not find suitable new premises in London, and it was decided to transfer the Guild and its activities to the village of Chipping Campden in Gloucestershire. About 150 people made the move.

The Chipping Campden adventure was much more than a response to a practical difficulty – it was in line with the whole philosophy that Ashbee and his colleagues professed. The attempt was made to turn Chipping Campden into a community on a new model, where the day's work was fully integrated with leisure activities and with opportunities for self-improvement. Local people were encouraged to participate, on an equal footing with the newcomers. Ashbee offered instruction in swimming, gardening, cookery and carpentry. He also organized Oxford University extension classes. An old photograph shows the guildsmen doing physical jerks in flat caps, starched shirts and stiff collars. Visitors who came down to see what was being done wrote glowing accounts of the rural utopia which the Guild had created in this beautiful Gloucestershire village.

But this migration to the country played a large part in destroying the Guild of Handicraft. Transport to London proved to be difficult and expensive; and, for the London clientele, out of sight was out of mind. In addition to this, the general economic climate was increasingly unfavorable. Ashbee, like Morris before him, was forced to recognize the paradox upon which the Guild's operations were based. There is more than a hint of bitterness in his verdict: "We have made of a great social movement, a narrow and tiresome little aristocracy working with great skill for the very rich." Even the very rich were unwilling to pay the true rate for the job. The craftsmen of the Guild increasingly suffered from the competition of the amateur whom Ashbee called "dear Emily," who was "tingling to sell her work before she half knows how to make it." By 1905 or 1906 the Guild of Handicraft was already in in very low water financially; in 1908 it had to be dissolved and reconstructed as a trust. In this form it struggled on until the outbreak of war in 1914.

Ashbee also resembles Morris in that he, too, suffered a change of heart about the machine. In 1911 we find him declaring that: "Modern civilization rests on machinery, and no system for the endowment, or the encouragement, or the teaching of art can be sound that does not recognize this." One reason for this change of mind seems to have been the impact upon Ashbee of Frank Lloyd

Wright. Ashbee met Wright in Chicago in December 1900. He looked at some of Wright's latest work, notably the just-completed Husser House, and was tremendously taken with his ideas as well as by his personality. In 1910 Wright stayed with the Ashbees in Chipping Campden, and in 1911 Ashbee supplied the introduction to the second Wasmuth edition of Wright's work, published in Berlin. The first edition had been strictly limited, so this was the form in which Wright's ideas first became generally available to the European public.

The contact between Wright and Ashbee was by no means the first example of a link between the English Arts and Crafts Movement and what was going on in America. Americans learnt about these new developments almost as soon as they began to gain impetus: for many the first, dazzling contact with them came thanks to Oscar Wilde's celebrated lecture tour in 1882. Even before this, the gospel preached by Morris had begun to gain a foothold. Louis Comfort Tiffany knew and admired what Morris had done. He founded his decorating firm in 1879 with Morris's example very much in mind. No brief account of the growth of the crafts movement prior to 1914 would be complete without some discussion of its impact upon the United States.

The first phase, which lasted until about 1893, saw a gradual but steady growth of interest in the crafts. 1880 was the date of the foundation of the Rookwood Pottery in Cincinnati which was to be so closely and so confusingly linked to the Women's Pottery Club in the same city. 1891 saw the re-foundation of an existing company, the Chelsea Keramic Art Works in Massachusetts, under the new name of the Chelsea Pottery. This, like Rookwood, produced wares which were recognizably craft-oriented.

The years 1893 to 1901 witnessed an extremely rapid expansion of craft activity. Numerous craft societies were founded. In 1894 the energetic Elbert Hubbard went to see William Morris at the Kelmscott Press and was so deeply fascinated that, on his return home, he bought a small press and printed an edition of the *Song of Songs,* the first book to bear the Roycroft colophon. From the press itself sprang the Roycroft bindery, then a leather shop, and by 1901 Hubbard was also selling simple, heavy craft furniture. In 1897 the first major crafts exhibition to be held in the United States was staged at Copley Hall, Boston. This was followed, later in the same year, by the foundation of the Boston Arts and Crafts Society and the Chicago Arts and Crafts Society, both modeled upon the London original. In January 1901, the Guild of Arts and Crafts of New York came into being.

From 1901 to 1916 the American craft movement apparently continued to flourish, and a new, more severely geometric style of ornamentation became popular, replacing the Art Nouveau-influenced patterns and forms which had been used before. *Craftsman* magazine established itself as the spokesman of a younger generation, Arts and Crafts ideas and artifacts were now widely disseminated among a modestly prosperous middle-class public. This was the time when the Roycroft community at East Aurora, New Jersey, was most active and successful. It was also the epoch at which Gustav Stickley and his brothers were distributing their "revolutionary" furniture all over America. It was dubbed revolutionary, not for any radical design innovation, but because its starkness contrasted almost brutally with the styles that had formerly been popular with more cultivated sections of the American middle class.

But, by achieving widespread popularity in both England and America, the crafts sowed the seeds of their own destruction. From being a crusade, they had declined into being merely a fashion; and in due time another fashion would come along to replace them. Moreover, the kind of taste they appealed to was being criticized from several quarters, and on several different levels. The most serious criticism, but not necessarily the most damaging, came from those in agreement with Thorstein Veblen, who in 1899 had already equated the hand-made object with conspicuous consumption. Veblen said:

> the visible imperfections of the hand-wrought goods, being honorific, are accounted marks of superiority in point of beauty, or serviceability, or both. Hence has arisen that exaltation of the defective, of which John Ruskin and William Morris were such spokesmen in their time; and on this ground their propaganda of crudity and wasted effort has been taken up and carried forward since their time.

Related to this attack was that launched by the new Futurist avant-garde, with its worship of the machine. Marinetti's declaration that "a racing automobile is more beautiful than the Victory of Samothrace" found its echoes in America (where in any case the machine had not altogether lost its prestige) just as it did elsewhere. The Armory Show of 1913, which gave wide publicity to Futurist ideas, sounded the death knell of the craft movement in America, just as it was the signal for a new beginning in painting and sculpture.

The most insidious, and as Ashbee had found in England, the most dangerous enemy of the crafts was, however, the rising interest in antiques. Nineteenth-century historicism had gradually transformed itself into a passion for what was called "the genuine article" (which was often not genuine at all). The efforts of the contemporary craftsman were dismissed as a debasement of what had been produced by his ancestors. It was the start of the craze for the complete period room, in which nothing was new, and nothing was out of keeping.

There are several observations to be made on the American incarnation of the Arts and Crafts Movement, and perhaps several lessons to be drawn from it. Despite Ashbee's denunciation of "dear Emily," it is in the United States that we see most clearly both the importance of the amateur and the involvement of women. The history of the Rookwood pottery is a case in point. This is a slightly complicated tale, but worth disentangling nonetheless.

In 1871 a young Cincinnati chemist called Karl Langenbeck was performing some experiments with a set of china-painting colors, which had been sent to him by an uncle in Frankfurt. He was joined in his experiments by a socially prominent young woman called Maria Longworth Nichols. In 1872, a class in china painting for Cincinnati's fashionable ladies was set up by one Benn Pitman, brother of the man who invented Pitman's shorthand. Among those who attended it was Mary Louise McLaughlin, daughter of the city's leading architect. By 1876, the members of Benn Pitman's class were skilled enough to send a display of their work to the Philadelphia Centennial Exposition. But of course they were working on ready-made blanks in over-glaze colors, and their work could therefore still be thought of as a genteel hobby, though one which they practiced with a good deal of skill and determination.

When the ladies visited the Exposition, they were particularly impressed by two things — the oriental ceramics, and a display of French barbotine ware. This was a process of underglaze decoration with colored slips. Miss McLaughlin determined to master it, and she succeeded. In 1878 the Women's Pottery Club was reorganized, with her as president. Mrs. Nichols was invited to join, but the invitation never reached her. The supposed snub caused hard feelings, and occasioned a certain degree of rivalry. But when Mrs. Nichols found her own working quarters at the Hamilton Road Pottery of a man named Frederick Dallas, the Club was forced to transfer its operations to the same place, as the situation in which they found themselves was unsatisfactory.

Mrs. Nichols, however, wanted to be independent. In 1880, she founded her own pottery in an abandoned schoolhouse. It was called "Rookwood" after the family estate, and also because the name seemed to carry an echo of Wedgwood. She was determined to put the enterprise on a sound business basis, and was happy to sell greenware to the Women's Pottery Club, and to fire it after it had been decorated. The two factions were thus for a time reconciled.

Rookwood wares soon became commercially successful, and their success had two consequences. One was that the pottery began to change from a place that produced studio work by amateurs to one that had a regularly employed staff of professional decorators. The other was that it spawned a number of imitators. Rival potteries, run on a purely commercial footing, sprang up elsewhere in Ohio. These imitators made wares of the same kind, but seldom, as it happened, with the same finesse.

As a consequence of Rookwood's growth, it soon had to close its doors to the amateurs. In 1883 the members of the Women's Pottery Club had to go back to the simpler method of over-glaze decoration on china, and were thus back exactly where they had started a decade before.

Even in bare outline, the story of the Rookwood pottery illustrates the dilemmas which faced the middle-class amateurs who were attracted to the craft movement, and who often developed a high degree of skill in their chosen métier. If they were at all serious, they could seldom remain wholly amateurs for long. The idea of skill as something therapeutic, an element necessary to the good life, could not stand against both the ambition and the practical need to make the craft activity self-supporting.

Not that this problem was unique to America. Stresses of the same kind can be detected in the life and work of the English potter, William de Morgan. De Morgan came from middle-class stock — his father was well known as a mathematician. The son trained at the Royal Academy Schools, and, after getting to know Morris, began to work as a craftsman in stained glass. Later he switched to being a decorator of tiles and pottery, bought unglazed but ready-made from Staffordshire manufacturers. Dissatisfied with this, he set up a pottery in Merton, Surrey, where he made his own wares and continued the experiments he had already started with Persian and luster glazes. De Morgan was now making what is perhaps the most splendid pottery produced in the course of the nineteenth century.

Yet he could not sustain the necessary level of effort, and was forced, stage by stage, to draw in his horns. In 1888 he moved to a pottery in Fulham, which was much closer to where he himself lived. In the 1890's his health started to deteriorate, and he began to spend his winters in Florence. He now worked by painting patterns on paper — these were afterwards transferred to tiles by an experienced staff of decorators. The same economic conditions as had affected Ashbee's enterprise in Chipping Campden now started to press upon de Morgan also, and in 1907 he at last had to close his pottery. During the last decade of his life he made an extremely successful new career for himself as a novelist, earning a great deal of money from his books. De Morgan reflected that the checks would have been more welcome had they arrived in time to save his business as a potter, for he was well aware that he had built up a unique fund of technical knowledge.

As we can see from these two outline histories, the first incarnation of the craft movement was involved, not only with the uncertain pattern of nineteenth-century economics, but with the class-system of the period. The story of the Guild of Handicraft is in many respects a cautionary tale which the modern craftsman would do well to heed. And the evolution of the movement in America raises in acute form the question of the pressures exercised by fashion, and of the dangers of fashionability. The craftsman found himself taken up by the public, sucked dry of any immediately assimilable ideas he might have, and then dropped again. Yet the Arts and Crafts Movement built up a substantial record of achievement, and we must remember that the achievement was based, not on an eye for the main chance, but on idealism,

This idealism was of two sorts: the nostalgic and the practical. The customers who brought temporary success to the Roycroft community and to the various enterprises operated by the Stickley brothers were expressing a longing for a different sort of life from the one the industrial revolution had given them, though they were of course unwilling to surrender the material benefits which it had conferred. On the other hand, men like Morris and Ashbee wanted to bring about a real change in society by changing men's attitudes toward their surroundings and toward the way in which useful objects were made. When they reached the United States, these ideas formed a direct link with the surviving remnant of the pioneer spirit.

We have no cause to mock the era in which Frances M. Glessner, one of the leaders of Chicago society, could note the following in her diary for the year 1905: "Thursday I went to the Fortnightly and took a silver dish of my own make as a present." The dish survives, and is a beautiful thing, original in design and finely finished. Mrs. Glessner stamped it with her personal mark — a G superimposed with a bee. The bee is a reference to another hobby of hers; she was an enthusiastic bee-keeper at the family's summer house in New Hampshire.

Bernard Leach, now in his eighties.

The contemporary craftsman is the direct descendant of the craftsmen of the nineteenth century, both in his rebellion against industrialism, and in his determination to live and work independently. There are also obvious personal connections. Bernard Leach, for example, had already begun his lifetime of devotion to the crafts before the First World War. Born in 1887, he studied at the Slade School in London under Henry Tonks (this was the artistic environment which produced Augustus John), and was given lessons in etching by Frank Brangwyn, that still-neglected master of English Symbolism. In 1909 Leach went to Japan to study with Shigekichi Ogata, sixth member of the Kenzan dynasty. In 1920 he returned to England, bringing with him his friend Shoji Hamada. They settled in St. Ives, Cornwall, and began the venture which continues with the Leach pottery of the present day. St. Ives has remained a point of pilgrimage for everyone interested in the crafts since Leach first established himself there.

In spring, the town he chose deserves all the adjectives that enthusiasts lavish upon it. Unlike the nearby Land's End, where the scenery has a mangy look, and the grass is worn away by the feet of thousands of tourists, St. Ives is spruce, dapper, and shows no sign of the invasion which will overwhelm it in the summer season. The Leach Pottery, however, is not in St. Ives itself but on the outskirts. Here the surroundings are less than picturesque. Facing it across the road are a garage and a gas station. Behind is a new housing development.

Above: The Leach Pottery, not as idyllic as it once was.

Opposite page: The Leach Pottery, the wood-fired kiln.

Things have changed in other ways as well. Leach is now an old man. The day-to-day running of the pottery is in the hands of his American wife, Janet. She regards the enterprise she has inherited with a mixture of wry scepticism and true devotion to the values it still represents. "By making this decision to establish himself in St. Ives," she says, "Bernard intuitively set a pattern for the twentieth-century artist-craftsman — live where you can *live*." But she immediately points out that the decision had an element of paradox about it even in the days when the town was less developed than it now is.

"Bernard built the first Oriental wood-fired climbing kiln to exist in the western hemisphere in an area where there are virtually no trees. And there's virtually no fire-clay here either, despite the Cornish china-clay industry." Yet the environment remains important: "Though the potter lives in a community that can't support him financially, and though he brings his material in, the community spirit supports him. The craftsman is opting out in order to opt in." She is, however, firmly resistant to romanticizing impulses. "I'm afraid the expectations of our visitors are still often governed by Bernard Leach's book of 1930. When they come to see us, they think we'll be having aesthetic discussions, or practicing the tea-ceremony."

As she shows me round, she talks about the way the pottery is organized. "All organizations develop expectations. And when you hear the baby crying, you pick it up. I inherited the group situation we all

Janet Leach, an American in England.

"Though the potter lives in a community that can't support him financially, and though he brings his material in, the community spirit supports him."

live within, but I'm not sure now that I would have formed it myself."

The Leach pottery is run by Janet Leach and her husband, but it is really a kind of cooperative where a number of potters work. Some, like William Marshall, have been there for a long time. He was a local boy who joined the pottery as a fourteen-year-old school-leaver. All, even the most junior members, are paid, and all are expected to make their contribution to the steady output of Leach standard-ware. In 1970 the pottery produced over 15,000 pieces of this, as opposed to some three or four hundred individual pots. Janet Leach sees the standard-ware not only as an economic basis for the business, but as the most effective way for a young potter to learn: "He throws a predetermined shape, but has a wide latitude for exploration within that shape. He must keep the image of making each batch better than the batch before, though he knows by the catalogue they will sell for the same price. While the potter is making a hundred mugs, he must always remember that one person is going to use one mug."

The idealism which is the motivating force of the Leach Pottery is based on a concept of the good life which goes back to Ruskin and Morris. Fundamental to this concept is a respect for the individual and a respect for the environment he lives in. But it can, of course, run into unexpected snags. I encountered an example of this on the day I visited it. The climbing kiln was being fired, and Janet leach was having anxious consultations about its

behavior. The smoke from the kiln is now a nuisance to the neighbors who crowd so thickly round, and a new method was being tried to make it consume more of its own waste products. The new method was unsuccessful: the smoke was not much diminished, and the kiln (as they told me) was firing more slowly than usual.

If Janet Leach has to face strictly practical problems connected with the running of the pottery, she also has to face others which concern her own personal development as a craftsman. Naturally, she finds her husband's influence difficult to escape. "I'm not sure," she says at one point, "how far I've found my identity outside Bernard." Yet the Leach tradition, within which she works, has given her a clear vision of what pots and pottery are about. She reacts sharply, for example, against the suggestion that she might think of herself as a kind of sculptor. "I don't like hybrids, sculpture-pots," she says. "I want pots or I want sculpture. Standards in pots have nothing to do with standards in sculpture. As it happens, I'm a potter who takes more interest in clays than in glazes. And I like kilns. I like fire. Fire's a very creative process. Getting involved with fire is what brought me to pottery."

Later on that same spring afternoon, she took me to see her husband. Bernard Leach used to live at his pottery, but has recently moved to a superb modern block of apartments on the water's edge in St. Ives. One of his daughters receives me and takes me upstairs to meet her father. Leach is seated by the wide picture window, which looks out over an

"All organizations develop expectations. And when you hear the baby crying, you pick it up"

immense panorama — the waves, the surfers and the gulls. The room is comfortable, tweedy, masculine. It reminds me of the headmaster's study at my first boarding school.

After apologizing for not coming to meet me (his eyesight is failing) he launches into a serious, passionate discourse. I am at once reminded of his wife's remark: "Now that he doesn't see so well, talk has become one of Bernard's art forms."

Obviously, it's impossible to recapture the whole of a discourse of this nature, but here are some excerpts from it:

On the relationship between the fine arts and the crafts: "There's a false difference. The idea of separation and division in art is a tedious, troublesome thing. One must simply judge by the amount of vitality in the work — we've at last reached a point where the painter is not to be feared. All efforts to resuscitate dead crafts have been a failure; what it now needs is an artist and a craftsman in one."

On craftsmanship itself: "The sign of good craftsmanship is leaving everything just so for the start of the next day. The good potter is like the good cook: he can look at the fire and know the color of white heat, accurately to within twenty degrees or so. Intellectual knowledge needs to be subdued by intuitional knowledge. The intellect can learn that it can think, rationally, from a basically intuitive background of animal life."

At this point he launches into a description of his lifelong friend Shoji Hamada decorating several

Above: Janet Leach and John Reeve discuss how the kiln is firing; they are trying a new method to reduce the smoke.

Below: An assistant tests the progress of firing in the wood-fired kiln.

hundred pots in the course of a day. The punch line of the story is Hamada's retort to the question of how he did it: "I asked the pot what it wanted, and gave it to it." My mind goes back to Janet Leach's description of her discovery of her own vocation as a potter. She was watching Hamada throw: "I took one look at him on the wheel and said; 'Aha! That's it.'"

Hamada's example is evidently never very far from Bernard Leach's own thoughts, for immediately after describing his friend's prowess as a decorator, he begins to talk about Japanese aesthetic attitudes. "They have an aversion to the word 'God'. What they speak of is 'thusness': the thing in its true nature. There is a Japanese word, *shibui,* which means noble, simple, heartfelt, non-luxurious. It means doing things, making things, using things in a way that hangs well for artists. Ephemeral art is not nonsense: art can be something that stings you, like a mosquito." It seems that he means by this last comment, not that pots themselves should be for a day's use only, but that certain gestures and attitudes of mind can have the force of art. The potter's life can therefore be an evolving aesthetic statement, and his smallest actions have significance. The Japanese have recongized this fact by designating certain craftsmen, among them Hamada himself, as National Living Treasures.

By this time the light is fading from the room and has almost left the beach and the sea outside, though there are still one or two surfers left. Mr.

Left: William Marshall throwing. Marshall is one of the best known potters working at the Leach Pottery. He is locally born and started there almost straight from school.

Below: John Reeve, another distinguished potter who has worked for long spells at the Leach Pottery.

"I'm a potter who takes more interest in clays than in glazes. And I like kilns. I like fire. Fire's a very creative process. Getting involved with fire is what brought me to pottery"

Leach is starting to look a little tired, and I begin to think that I am outstaying my welcome. But he is reluctant to let me leave. Talking more slowly now, and almost as if to himself, he says: "How was this given to me? It wasn't me, but some other power at work. Below the levels of our consciousness, we can communicate with other levels of consciousness."

This description of the Leach Pottery, and of the two chief personalities connected with it, rightly stands at the beginning of an attempt to describe, by means of a series of examples, the contemporary craftsman and his situation. In point of time, Leach preceded all the rest; and because he has been a prolific writer, his ideas have formed the basis for discussion among young craftsmen, who either accept them or react against them. In addition to this, Leach has created the image of the craftsman which now exists in the public mind. It is largely due to him that pottery is now the most popular form of craft expression. It is also the one whose aesthetics have been most fully worked out. From talking to potters one sees very clearly not only the various conflicts which beset the contemporary craftsman, but the alternatives he has and the opportunities which are offered to him.

If one tries to strip away some of the mythical accretions which have grown up around Leach and his pottery — and I do this in a spirit of admiration and gratitude rather than of criticism — one sees that it stands at the head of a number of warring traditions or streams of development. Three of these in particular seem to call for comment. One is a

43

matter which relates to the modern crafts taken as a whole, the other two are more specifically linked to ceramics.

The first of these is a demonstration of the craftsman's way of life as a demonstration of belief in certain moral principles. Even though the Leach Pottery shelters a number of first-rate potters, it retains its hold on the public imagination less for this reason than for the ideal of life it is thought to typify. The reaction of many visitors must be "if only I could live like that!" Those connected with it are keenly conscious that it possesses this role, and they are sometimes puzzled about how to adapt Bernard Leach's original ideas to modern conditions. For the world in which his pottery now exists and struggles for survival is very different from the world in which he founded it.

Many of the other craftsmen I interviewed are worried that Leach has laid upon his juniors and successors a command to be moral exemplars to the society that surrounds them.

On another level, one finds a declared or undeclared opposition among young potters to Leach's aesthetic and technical ideas. They criticize Leach because they find in his work too slavish an attachment to the Oriental and especially the Japanese tradition. Of course, this is not the case with Janet Leach herself. She describes her own real education as a potter as having begun when she paid her first visit to Japan in the spring of 1954. She has gone there often since.

It is true that the Leach aesthetic also

Above: Bernard Leach in full spate. His wife thinks talking "is one of his art forms."

Right: Janet Leach in the drying room, where the pots are put to dry before being glazed and fired.

44

"The idea of separation and division in art is a tedious, troublesome thing. One must simply judge by the amount of vitality in the work — we've at last reached a point where the painter is not to be feared"

Above: Bernard Leach, still in full spate.

Opposite page: Typical of Bernard Leach's best recent work — a tall vase showing strong Oriental influence. Leach is celebrated among potters for the power of his brushwork.

incorporates a passionate admiration for certain kinds of English medieval pottery, which is liked for qualities which seem to relate it to the Japanese idea of instinctive response to the qualities of clay and the motion of the wheel — it is as much the product, according to this school of thought, of a "right" attunement to the forces to be found within nature as anything produced by Japan herself.

Another important characteristic of the Leach Pottery — but one which has attracted less discussion — is its status as a small manufactory. All discussion of craft pottery tends to be confused by the fact that we often don't know whether the wares we are discussing are produced in order to be used, or whether their purpose is primarily aesthetic. Part of this confusion arises from our attitudes toward the ceramics which have been produced in the past. Many objects which were undoubtedly designed to serve a useful purpose have been translated, by age and value, into honored positions in a museum showcase or collector's cabinet. Craftsmen, attracted by what they see in museums, sometimes tend to produce modern "museum-pieces" in flat contradiction to their own declared purpose. But the danger chiefly arises that the craftsman will settle for a compromise, and that his works will turn out to be not-quite-functional and too-good-to-be-used — but nevertheless will not qualify as collector's objects.

From the point of view of those who run it, the artistic as well as the financial foundation of the Leach enterprise is the large output of wares which are designed for everyday use. As Janet Leach

"The intellect can learn that it can think, rationally, from a basically intuitive background of animal life"

implies, the discipline involved in making what is useful makes possible the creation of more ambitious work, in which beauty is the principal aim.

While the Leach Pottery is not unique in producing a range of standard-ware, enterprises of this kind are increasingly in the minority. I visited two others, both significantly different from what I found in St. Ives. One point of interest about them is that they represent successive generations of craft activity, since one was founded in the nineteen-fifties and the other in the nineteen-sixties.

Alan Caiger-Smith is, among those with an enthusiasm for ceramics, now almost as well known as Bernard Leach himself, though his work springs from a very different tradition. His Aldermaston Pottery is today more beautifully situated than the Leach Pottery. It is to be found in a Berkshire village.

Caiger-Smith began the venture in 1955. The location chose itself: he bought a run-down group of farm buildings opposite the house where his mother was living. For a year he worked by himself but since then he has always had assistance. The specialty of the pottery is tin-glazed earthenware. The intensely individual style of the work it produces must, despite the number of people who work there, be referred directly to Caiger-Smith himself. It stems from his own training as a painter, and also from the "moment of recognition" which made him decide to become a potter. This happened when, as a young man on a yachting holiday, he sailed up the Guadalquivir River in Spain and saw traditional

Above: Bernard Leach can also ask sudden, disconcerting questions when he is being interviewed.

Opposite page: A self-caricature by Leach. It shows him, his wife says, "pulling all the bad potters along."

49

Alan Caiger-Smith decorating
a bowl at the Aldermaston
Pottery.

"How was this given to me? It wasn't me, but some other power at work. Below the levels of our consciousness, we can communicate with other levels of consciousness"

Spanish potters at work in the city of Seville.

The Aldermaston Pottery is not a cooperative even in the sense that the Leach Pottery is. Caiger-Smith does not supply all the designs, but he does create most of them. Those which are not his must nevertheless fit the "personality" of the rest of the range. This covers a wide variety indeed – mugs, casseroles, plates, bowls, tiles. There are purely practical pieces produced in series, and others are produced as special items.

At Aldermaston there is no abrupt division between the purely utilitarian and pieces where the aesthetic impulse predominates. One category shades into the next by imperceptible degrees, yet Caiger-Smith avoids the danger of a conflict between the decorative and the useful. Nearly everything made at the pottery fulfils a specific function, and often the pieces are designed to do a particular job in a particular way. "We often get ideas," Caiger-Smith says, "from the fact that people come to us and say 'Can you make me so-and-so?' The range keeps on growing and growing, but then in the end you have to trim it down. Then, again, there's the problem of certain items we can always sell, but which you get bored and stale with making over and over again. If we made nothing but casseroles, we could still sell them all."

He points out that special orders, though fun to carry out, may not always be to the advantage of the pottery, because they can disrupt the even flow of work. "You have to decide between the personal

relationship, and what's good for the business. Of course, if you really like the person, you always try to do it."

He has strong views about how the teamwork of a pottery such as his ought to be organized. There is usually no question of dividing what has to be done (though this, arguably, might be more efficient) so that one person throws, another paints, another packs the kilns and sees to the firing. They each carry through a particular job from first to last, and try to share the interruptions brought by visitors and necessary but boring jobs such as packing.

Among other potters, and indeed other craftsmen in general, Caiger-Smith is famous for his gifts as a painter of pots. He allowed me to watch him decorate a series of bowls, and this was almost more instructive than his talk. In addition to tin-glaze, he has another specialty, which is luster-decoration. This puts him firmly in the tradition of William de Morgan, though he says that he knew little about de Morgan until comparatively recently. The fascination with a luster, like his story about sailing up the Guadalquivir, may illustrate a romantic streak in his character: the process is notoriously difficult, and the results are almost impossible to predict. Caiger-Smith says that when he first tried it they had twenty-four successive firings without producing luster at all.

The pieces to be painted on the day of my visit were to be luster-decorated. Picking up each in turn, he signed it and set it on a small turntable on his workbench. Turning the piece round as he worked,

51

Above: The Aldermaston Pottery – everyone takes a particular job and follows it through.

Right: Casserole lids must fit properly. This is one way of making sure they do.

Opposite page: One of Caiger-Smith's young assistants pauses for a moment before making the first, decisive stroke on a bowl awaiting decoration.

he covered the inner surface with a series of rapid, powerful arabesques. Then he would squat down to decorate the outside. Occasionally, dissatisfied with what he had done, he would wipe the surface clean and start again. No bowl seemed to take him more than a few minutes. The decoration often seemed to unfurl like a flower unfolding its petals. As Caiger-Smith completed a bowl, he would tell me about the considerations which had prompted him to choose that particular type of decoration. Some kinds of luster "flash" in the firing — that is, the luster tends to tinge the whole of the surrounding glaze — and this calls for careful adjustment of the calligraphy.

Later he talked, now more eloquently, about decoration in general: "I think it's a horrid word. The great danger of tin-glaze pottery is ephemeral and unneccessary surface-decoration. If you only paint, you become a virtuoso, and forget that what you paint belongs to a form. The painting and the form ought to be one thing — inseparable." Then, reverting to the question of private commissions: "I think it's a pity that most modern craftsmen seem to be rather frightened of their clients. It means something to get to know the person — the whole exchange between the two of you. Yet there must, in the end, be a limit to the private commissions you can take. The moment comes when you don't have time to do it properly, and that's when you do it without joy."

It is this final remark that links Aldermaston Pottery most closely to the situation I found at St.

Ives. Yet it must be admitted that Caiger-Smith's situation, too, raises a number of questions about the craftsman's responsibility to himself and to others, to which different answers have been given by other people, notably by the independent potters whose attitudes are described in the next chapter. His method of operation, for instance, embodies a constant if subdued conflict between what is good for the business and what is good for the individual. Many younger potters have avoided this by considering themselves pure artists, and not having a business in this sense at all.

The position of the craftsman as a member of a team, and his precise relationship to the patron who commissions him, should be given more attention than has hitherto come their way. The closer the crafts draw to the situation and the aesthetic principles which prevail in so-called fine art, the less acceptable the notion of teamwork, at least as Caiger-Smith defines it, becomes to the young craftsman. Yet an enterprise such as the Aldermaston Pottery could not operate except on this basis – the subordination of a number of people to the vision of one man. There is a comparison to be drawn here with the studio practice of Renaissance and Baroque painters. Sometimes, as with the young Leonardo when he was Verrocchio's apprentice, the pupil will surpass the master, and gradually draw away from him. This is a process we can see happening in the *Baptism* in the Uffizzi. Even though the painting is a product of Verrocchio's studio, the intervention of Leonardo's

personal handwriting gradually grows more
apparent, not to say obtrusive, the longer we look at
it. But often Leonardo is content to make an
anonymous contribution, as is the case with nearly
all of Rubens's assistants. Caiger-Smith's
co-workers seem very happy with the situation he
provides for them, and he receives many
applications for jobs at the pottery that he is forced
to turn down.

The patron and his relationship to the man
whom he patronizes is another tricky question, and
Alan Caiger-Smith gave me one of the clearest
statements I received about the problems involved.
One might think, for instance, that one obvious way
for the craftsman to survive in contemporary society
is by supplying needs which industry is not flexible
enough to deal with.

Yet the patron's demands, as we have seen, can
actually upset the economic basis of the craftsman's
enterprise. In addition, by venturing too far in his
suggestions and demands, he can upset the
craftsman's personal equilibrium, his feeling of
self-fulfillment. No craftsman really likes being used
as the channel for the blocked creative impulses
which the patron himself, through circumstances or
lack of talent, has been unable to fulfil. The potter
insists on retaining aesthetic as well as economic
self-sufficiency.

"Self-sufficiency," indeed, is perhaps the keynote
of my description of the potter who occupies the
third and final place in this chapter. Alan
Caiger-Smith and Emmanuel Cooper are a contrast

"There must, in the end, be a limit to the private commissions you can take. The moment comes when you don't have time to do it properly, and that's when you do it without joy"

in appearance, just as they are a contrast in background. Caiger-Smith might be a soldier turned country squire. He was educated at Cambridge, though he subsequently attended art school. Cooper's background is working-class, and he attended the Royal College of Art.

Watching Cooper throw is almost as instructive as watching Caiger-Smith decorate. He is a lithe, muscular man, all of whose movements have a certain stylishness. In respose he stretches out, cat-like, or folds his legs under him in the lotus position. His clothes, too, are stylish — beautifully fitted washed-out denims which combine practicality with an air of sly raffishness. When he sits down to throw, however, much of this alters. He puts on a striped apron, prepares the clay, breaks it into equal-sized lumps which he weighs on a scale, then begins to shape one of the lumps on the wheel. His casual physical elegance drops almost imperceptibly away. The body of a teapot is formed, cut away from the wheel, and put on a board. Another lump of clay replaces it. Later the lid will be made, plus the spout and the lugs that take the handle. Spout and lugs will be stuck to the body with slip. At another wheel in the background, Cooper's assistant Hassan is performing much the same series of operations, though he, as it happens, is making a series of large casseroles.

All of this takes place in a long tunnel-like room of a house in a rather grimy part of North London. There is no reason for the pottery to be situated where it is, except that it is a district where rents are

low, and Cooper finds London a good place to live. The firing is done in an electric kiln in another room on the same floor, and Cooper and Hassan both have flats above the pottery.

In the showroom, Cooper shows me some of the pots he makes in addition to his range of domestic ware. It is these — mostly bowls with subtle, Japanese-influenced glazes — which appear in exhibitions. The domestic pieces made at the Fonthill Pottery (it is named after the road in which it stands) sell like hot cakes in the kind of shop that promotes the simple life.

"You realize, of course," he says, "that what we make is a luxury product, not a rustic product. But then we live in a sophisticated society. The justification of my work is still that you can use it. I

"Simplicity is the appeal of pottery — particularly to people who aren't at all simple themselves"

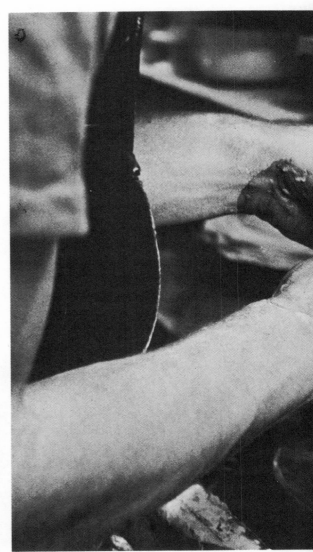

The body of a teapot grows on the wheel, under Emmanuel Cooper's skilful hands.

make things which you can use if you wish to, but which you can also like and admire. Simplicity is the appeal of pottery – particularly to people who aren't at all simple themselves."

Cooper uses the Fonthill Pottery as the basis for a complex range of different activities: teaching; running *Ceramic Review,* an influential craft magazine, from his flat upstairs; keeping in touch with what is happening in ceramics throughout the world. More than most of his colleagues, he could fairly be classified as a "craft intellectual." He himself sees it differently. "I'm being wildly self-indulgent," he says, "doing exactly what I want to do."

It isn't this, however, which makes him something of a new phenomenon as a craft-potter. Rather, it is his working-class background. Cooper claims, only half-jokingly, that his mother, whenever she calls him up to see how he is doing, asks not: "Emmanuel, are you well?" but "Emmanuel, have you got plenty of work?"

For him the Fonthill Pottery represents liberation of a very practical kind: freedom from the restricted circumstances in which he was brought up, and a transformation of the joyless and rigid Noncomformist work ethic into something which suits himself. The emphasis is still on self-help and on success through one's own efforts. Success, however, is not defined as a distant and abstract salvation. Rather, it consists in making the fullest use of one's own human potentialities in the world one happens to inhabit.

Lucie Rie is one of the most famous and best-respected of British studio potters. Her work can be seen in museums all over the world.

In a general sense it would be fair to say that the craftsman potter, working on his own as an individual artist, is now closer to representing the norm of the activity. Of all the potters working in "studio" conditions, on their own and without assistants, the two most celebrated names, at least in England, are probably those of Lucie Rie and Hans Coper.

Lucie Rie was born in Vienna and came to England as an already experienced studio potter in 1938. Soon after her arrival in England, she moved into the premises in London which she still occupies, with her workplace beneath and living quarters above. It is now a highly fashionable and desirable address, but must have been much less so when she arrived. The outbreak of war called a halt to her work, and she was not able to start again as a potter until 1945-6. In the postwar period she supported herself by making ceramic buttons and necklaces and a certain quantity of useful wares. It was at this time that Hans Coper, then a young German refugee who knew nothing about ceramics, came to work as her assistant. Rie and Coper still have a tremendous admiration for one another's work; Miss Rie's living quarters have numerous superb Coper pots on display, but none of her own.

Coper, after a period teaching at the Royal College of Art, has now moved to the country and lives, with his wife Jane, in rural isolation. The rustic quality of his surroundings is enhanced by the livestock — including three very personable nanny goats — wandering around his small property. The

Above: Lucie Rie's famous
chocolate biscuits —
something all her visitors
remember. On the table is a
pot by Hans Coper, the living
potter she most admires.

Opposite page: Hans
Coper's peaceful house in
Somerset.

"I like the dialectical method I find in nature. My patterns are based on overlapping systems"

contrast between Coper's environment and the one which Miss Rie has chosen for herself could hardly be more extreme.

Sadly, from my point of view, Miss Rie and Mr. Coper share an objection to being quoted. While both agreed to talk with me, gave generously of their time, they forbade me to print any directly attributed remark or opinion. In addition to this, Mr. Coper asked me not to photograph him, though he allowed me to document his studio. Yet these encounters with Lucie Rie and Hans Coper were important for a number of reasons. Because they were "off the record," both potters were extremely frank about their attitudes to their own work, and it was useful to have these remarks as a yardstick to measure my reactions to what was said to me upon other occasions.

In both cases, it was wise to look as well as to listen. Miss Rie's studio contains an immense accumulation of her own bowls and vases – pieces kept either because she especially likes them, or because she feels that she is unlikely to be able to repeat some effect of glaze. The repetition of shapes and colors, paradoxically, taught one to recognize that each vase and bowl of hers has a life and personality of its own. This impression of the "livingness" of her work was reinforced by a chance circumstance. On a table in the middle of the studio was a group of pieces newly taken from the kiln, and still in the process of cooling. As they cooled, they produced a series of musical notes. Our conversation was punctuated by sonorous "pings,"

Hans Coper's wife Jane, and their pet goats. The goats are strong-minded characters and the household has to pay a lot of attention to them.

as if the pots themselves were striving to find utterance and to enter in to what was being said.

Hans Coper, too, had quite a number of his own pieces to show me. Here there was much less variety of color and glaze: Coper basically only uses two glazes, a black and an off-white. Therefore, it was the shapes themselves that riveted the attention. Coper's work exemplifies the tendency, often found in modern studio pottery, for ceramics to aspire to the condition of sculpture.

Though his pots do not lose their character as vessels, they can hardly be described any longer as objects of use. But can they be thought of as the "sculpture-pots" that Janet Leach condemns? To my mind, they are not a compromise with the sculptural impulse, but something quite different. Coper's forms are based upon repetition, and upon the discipline imposed by the technique of throwing clay upon a wheel. One can see the basic nature of his work by looking at the accumulation of pots he has in his studio. There are shelves full of vessels of similar shape, all of them attempts at some unattainable formal ideal. The potter uses the same basic idea again and again, and each pot he makes is simultaneously a unique statement and an approximation to something the potter has in his mind's eye.

Coper never takes technical experiment so far that he loses all sense of the piece as a container. He often thrusts a dried flowerhead into one of his vases, and it in no way detracts from the eloquence of the statement made by the piece itself. When I

66

"I want people to be satisfied with the vessel just as they would be with sculpture"

visited her, Lucie Rie was using one of her Coper pots as a container for a trailing spray of orchids, and the flowers and the pot enhanced one another. Though a piece by Coper may look assymetrical, it has its roots in regularity – the regular rhythm of the wheel that was used to create it. The development in three dimensions is never completely free and unfettered by rules. These restraints are a gain rather than a loss. Pottery, in the hands of the modern craftsman, can offer many of the creative advantages of sculpture, but has others peculiar to itself. Coper's crowded shelves offer a more complete statement about his thinking process than the random accumulation one discovers in the studios of most artists. The implication is that the thinking process itself is more coherent because its boundaries are to some extent known.

Rie and Coper represent what may be said to be the dominant tradition in contemporary studio ceramics, which is that of the individual craftsman working on his own, inventing his own processes and pursuing his own formal and technical experiments. Some of the most important characteristics of their work are also to be found in that of studio potters of a younger generation. For example, both Rie and Coper have an eclectic relationship with ancient civilizations. Miss Rie does not identify herself with the Oriental tradition to nearly the same extent as Bernard Leach. Nonetheless, one can see the effect that Sung porcelains and stonewares in particular have had on her sensibility. It comes as no surprise to find a

Left: Lucie Rie will not allow herself to be quoted, but these pictures give some idea of the flavor of her talk.

Above: In Lucie Rie's studio. The pieces on the table have just been taken from the kiln and are still cooling.

splendid Korean stoneware jar among the objects in her studio.

Coper's pots, on the other hand, hint at influences derived from Egyptian pre-dynastic wares and from Cycladic art. In this sense, he is a product of the *musée imaginaire* which André Malraux was the first to describe, though it had existed ever since the invention of the lavishly-illustrated art book.

In the ceramics made by younger studio potters who have been influenced by Coper, such as Elizabeth Fritsch, one seems to detect an even more complex web of influences. Indeed, unraveling this web is part of the pleasure to be derived from looking at their work. Painting and sculpture have always been able to rely on this power of association. European art is rich in symbols, such as the skull and the hourglass of the *Vanitas* still life. More than this, painters from the Renaissance onwards have often been happy to rely on our memory of other works of art. We find a figure from a classical sarcophagus inserted into a composition by Ingres, and know that the painter means us to recognize its source. Similarly, the new generation of potters seem consciously to rely on our knowledge of other cultures.

There is another and very different point to be made about the new generation of studio potters, and this is that a disproportionately large number of the most gifted are women. Why does society view pottery as an "acceptable" career for a woman? It is too simplistic, I think, to assert that pottery arouses less resentment because it is still considered

Opposite page: On Hans Coper's desk — two of his favorite pots. They illustrate the two types of glaze he uses.

Above: Hans Coper's studio — a modern building next to his ancient stone house. He spends many hours there every day.

71

When Elizabeth Fritsch saw this picture she said, "Yes, I often feel like that!"

somehow inferior to the fine arts — inferior and by definition domestic. There may, of course, be an element of that. But one curious comparison which comes to mind is that between pottery and the novel. Novels, too, are creative territory where the male does not resent the incursion of the female. Despite all the radical and even scandalous novels that have been written, novel-writing as an activity is considered harmless, no challenge to male supremacy. And there is also perhaps an underlying notion that pots themselves are female things, receptive wombs for whatever we may care to put into them.

This idea might well appeal to Elizabeth Fritsch, who describes herself as being intensely interested in mythology in general, and more particularly in the archetypes in nursery rhymes. "Have you noticed," she says, "how often those rhymes seem to mention bags and pockets? As soon as I start to think about them, I start wanting to make pots."

At the time when I interviewed her, Miss Fritsch was living and working at an old manor house in Suffolk. Gelsingthorpe Hall is one of those buildings that give the English countryside its special flavor. The front is finely-proportioned early Georgian. Inside, the house straggles back, and still further back, with a series of additions built at later periods. Eventually one reaches the room Miss Fritsch is using as a studio. Glass-roofed, time- and water-stained, it is crammed with an amazing collection of objects: pots, toys, seashells, Chinese drawings and musical instruments. A straw hat

hangs jauntily from a bed-post, ribbons trailing.

Elizabeth Fritsch was born in 1940. Her parents are Welsh, and two of her aunts are bardic harpists, which explains the fact that she went to the Royal College of Music to study the harp with the famous harpist Ossian Ellis. "But," she says, "I was already torn betwen the visual arts and music. I tended to go to the museums instead of practicing." After her time as a music student, she did a teacher's course in Birmingham. It was here that she got her first taste of clay. A little later, now married and pregnant, she started making hand-built pots on the kitchen table.

Having arrived at her vocation in this unorthodox but, in her own mind at least, perfectly logical way, she applied as a late entrant to the Royal College of Art and was refused. With great determination, she applied again the following year, chiefly, she says, because she felt she had something important to learn from Hans Coper. This time she was accepted. She did a two-year degree course; and, this time without any financial aid, a third, postgraduate year. "It was very difficult," she says, "but I'm optimistic about money just as I'm optimistic about time." It must have been even more difficult than she admits, as somewhere along the line there had been a broken marriage, and she had her son as well as herself to support.

The interview took place at a kind of crisis-point in Elizabeth Fritsch's career. Eighteen months previously, she had returned to England from Denmark, having thrown up a job with a big ceramic firm in Copenhagen because she so much

Opposite page: Elizabeth Fritsch painting one of her pots. She uses engobe, not glaze, for decoration.

Above left: Some pots by Elizabeth Fritsch await painting. Since the decoration has to be precise, she first sketches the outlines in pencil.

Above: Elizabeth Fritsch's son Bertie likes to sit and watch his mother at work.

Glenys Barton (left) and
Jacqueline Poncelet (right)
share a studio in a London
railway arch.

disliked the working conditions she found there.
Now she was just in the last stages of preparation
for her first one-man show in London. Perhaps for
this reason, one was aware of a powerful current of
ideas, generated by the imminence of the show.
Making new pots had prompted a rethinking of her
attitudes toward pottery.

"I'm interested in nature," she says, "but I don't
want to copy appearances just the way things
happen . . . I like the dialectical method I find in
nature. My patterns are based on overlapping
systems." She picks up one of her pots to show me
what she means. Like the rest of her work it is
hand-built stoneware. The complex patterns are
painted in slip, fired but not glazed. They suggest
Pre-Columbian influence, just as the shapes
themselves seem to hint at Minoan pottery. It is as if
history had gone back in its tracks to create an extra
civilization, unknown till now, and this pot is part of
the evidence.

As she turns the vessel round in her hand, Miss
Fritsch is talking about the way in which she wants
it to work, to be received by the intended audience.
"I want people to be satisfied with the vessel just as
they would be with sculpture. But, as you see, it's
not really meant to be used. It has what I call a
purely 'surrealistic' use." To reinforce the point, she
has recently made a series of pieces in what she calls
"two-and-a-half dimensions." Looked at frontally,
which is the way they are meant to be viewed, these
pots look like fully rounded, symmetrical vessels.
Viewed from any other angle, they look like what

76

they are – a kind of perspective drawing in clay. "As you can see," she adds, "I like playing games with space."

It is clear that for her, the finished pot acquires a personality and identity quite separate from herself. "I like the texture," she remarks, "to be tending towards skin – human skin." Again, talking about form, she says: "All my forms are made to fit in the hand. They're not fully functional when they stand on a table – you have to pick it up. Put on the table, they try to be airborne."

We do not spend the whole day in her studio, but walk in the garden, have drinks with Miss Fritsch's hostess, and eat together in a huge farmhouse-style kitchen. Her son Bertie (named after the philosopher Bertrand Russell) plays with his toys, but when his mother starts to decorate the pots which are still unfinished, he wants to participate too. They sit at her worktable together. At one point she remarks, almost at a tangent: "If money grew on trees, I'd make pots anyway. I think I'd like to give them to friends, or even just to other people. I make pots as love-tokens." She pauses, reflectively: "But since one has to have money, I think I'd like to be nationalized, and sell only to the State. It's selling to individuals that I find alienating."

Glenys Barton and Jacqueline Poncelet are close friends – and friends and admirers of Elizabeth Fritsch's. Their working circumstances, however, are very different from hers – as different as Lucie Rie's are from Hans Coper's. They share a cramped little workshop slotted into a railway arch behind

Opposite page: One of these arches houses the place where Glenys Barton and Jacqueline Poncelet do most of their work.

Above: Glenys Barton trained as a dancer.

Right above: Glenys Barton at work in the back porch of her house in London. She is polishing a piece of marble which will be used as a base.

Right Below: A sheet of transfers. Glenys Barton has these specially made for her.

Below: Jacqueline Poncelet relaxes at home.

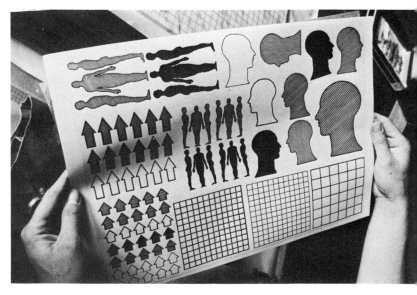

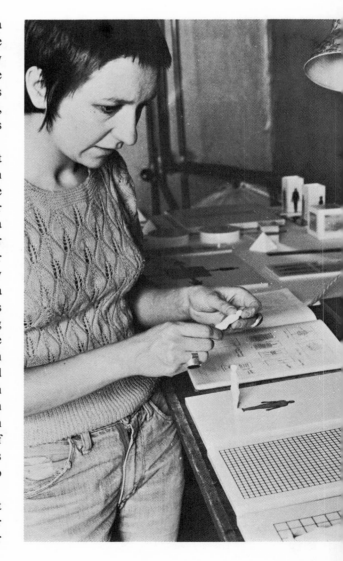

one of the big London stations. They find sharing a workshop convenient because they both work in the same medium — bone china. Working closely together, they do not collaborate, but keep complete freedom to criticize one another's work. "She bitches at me, and I bitch at her," Miss Poncelet says, smiling, while Glenys Barton nods vigorous agreement.

What they do is completely different in style, just as their backgrounds are different. Glenys Barton comes from Stoke-on-Trent, the center of the commercial ceramic industry in England. Her background is working-class — her father was a miner, later disabled; her mother was a hand-painter on china; her aunts are gilders. In some ways her entry into the crafts resembles the course taken by Elizabeth Fritsch. She started off by training as a teacher, though she admits that she nevertheless "did pottery all the time" and treated the training college "as if it were an art school." At the same time, she did a lot of dance and movement. When her training was completed she came to London and taught at Risinghill, a famous and famously tough London comprehensive school. After about eighteen months of this she had a nervous breakdown. When she recovered, she worked in the Institute of Education at London University as a potter's assistant, and at the same time taught pottery to housewives.

Her entry to the Royal College of Art came at the comparatively late age of twenty-five, after someone from the College had seen her pots more or

80

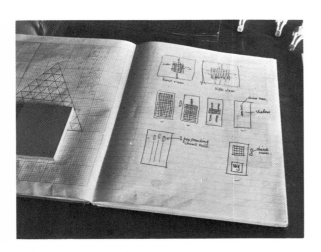

Left: Glenys Barton has a workroom in her own house, where she works on new ideas.

Above: One of Glenys Barton's notebooks. This is the way most of her projects begin.

less by accident. She had what she describes as "a stormy interview" and was accepted.

When she entered the RCA she wanted to be an industrial designer. And it soon looked as if she would succeed in this ambition. While she was still a student she designed a range of domestic china for the fashionable department store Habitat. This was accepted and put into production — the fulfilment of every ambitious student's dream, as she now points out. Yet midway through her course she rebelled against the future she had mapped out for herself.

Trying to explain this change of heart, she remarked to me that she couldn't accept the compromises which a career in industrial design seemed to involve — the perpetual concessions to the profit motive and, perhaps worse than this, the lack of imagination among commercial manufacturers.

Yet, when she decided that she would, after all, have to make a career by working on her own, she discovered that she couldn't go back to where she had begun. She had lost a certain kind of innocence: "After making precise models I couldn't go back to using clay as I'd used it before." Reinforcing this statement, she describes the excitement she felt when she first encountered switch boxes made in electro-porcelain. "Factory-made," she says, producing an example for me to look at, "and accurate to a thou." Then she adds: "Clay can be either soft or hard. I only discovered its hardness through industrial porcelain."

Today Glenys Barton is a ceramic sculptor, and her work increasingly tends to be shown in art

Top: Back at the workshop, Glenys Barton grinds a disc of bone china. She likes her work to be absolutely precise.

Bottom: Jacqueline Poncelet working on a mold. Her work is molded, not thrown. Variations in form arise from the effect of firing on the bone china she uses.

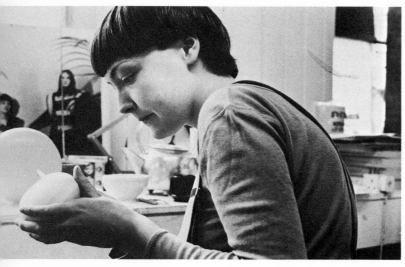

galleries rather than craft-shops. She describes herself as "forcing the material to an extreme, as far as it will go, as a reaction to the sloppiness of studio pottery." This reaction finds expression in quite a number of different ways, ranging from the decision to combine ceramic with other materials such as polished metal, to the fierce inscription written on the wall of her subsidiary studio at home. "Avoid surface decoration," it reads. "At all costs avoid craft!" Even if her current technical procedures do avoid craft as it is traditionally defined, they are often exceedingly laborious. They involve grinding and polishing the fired material in order to get rid of its natural tendency to distortion.

Questioned about her influences, Glenys Barton names, not other potters, but the sculptor and printmaker Eduardo Paolozzi. A course with Paolozzi was, she says, very important to her when she was a student at the RCA. He invited those attending it to construct their own kit of images, and encouraged their interest in the invention of "synthetic worlds." Miss Barton connects her fascination with Paolozzi's way of thinking with the pleasure she gets from avant-garde science fiction, notably J. G. Ballard's *Terminal Beach*.

Jacqueline Poncelet uses the same material as Glenys Barton, but employs it in a very different fashion. Her bone china pieces are cast in molds and are very light, thin and fragile. One might fairly compare some of them to nautilus shells. One of the means she uses to get color is through the use of colored stains in the paste.

"Forcing the material to an extreme, as far as it will go, as a reaction to the sloppiness of studio pottery"

Instead of combating the tendency of the material to distort in the kiln, Miss Poncelet tends to regard this as a necessary, if not wholly predictable part of the creative process. She describes it as "trying to get the end product you've imagined and getting the extra bonus of what you haven't imagined." At first hearing, this sounds like an extension of the comment which Janet Leach made: "The difference between being a potter and a fine artist is that as a potter you've got to accept what the fire gives you."

But one remembers, too, the interest taken by certain modern artists in chance procedures, and also the aleatory element in a good deal of modern music. Submission to the given is not necessarily something characteristic of potters alone. It may, instead, represent a general commitment to the modernist ethos.

Despite this reliance on chance and on accidental effects, Miss Poncelet's techniques involve an amount of intellectual and physical effort which is perhaps belied by the delicacy of the result. She describes herself as "only happy when I'm learning: if I feel I'm feeding off things I already know, I get very moody about it." Her work is a constant process of rethinking, and the thought does not necessarily move in only one direction at a time. She returns to old ideas "just to make sure I haven't abandoned them because I wasn't willing to put myself out." She likes exhibitions but also dreads them: not only do they give her a sense of purpose, something to work toward, but they are "a way of

judging." She adds that she doesn't much like selling through shops "because my work needs to be considered."

The interesting thing about these remarks, especially if one takes them in conjunction with those made by Elizabeth Fritsch, is the degree to which they relate the potter's work to the climate prevailing in the fine arts. In the case of Glenys Barton the direction her recent work has taken has made her yet more keenly aware, if possible, of this relationship than Poncelet and Fritsch. It was she who urged Jacqueline Poncelet to ask me to dinner, so that I could see, as she said, "how Jackie lives with her own things." The pretty room did, as she promised, contain a curious selection of objects: seashells (all potters seem to love these), kitsch items in plastic and ceramic, birds' eggs, a bright feather, a toy robot. All of these dwelt together in perfect congruity as the perhaps unconscious, and certainly unselfconscious, portrait of the sensibility of the occupant. It was a sensibility that could be described as being at once post-Surrealist and post-Pop, and it sent me back to Miss Poncelet's ceramics with new eyes.

How far do all three of the potters whom I have just described depart from the traditional notion of craft, at least as it applies in their field? Not one of the three makes any use of the wheel, and if the hand-building technique used by Elizabeth Fritsch has an extremely ancient history, then it must be admitted that she uses it for highly original ends.

Bone china, the preferred medium of Miss

83

Poncelet and Miss Barton, is a product of the Industrial Revolution of the nineteenth century, It has hitherto been associated with a factory, rather than a craft situation. But the two potters concerned use it without reference to industrial techniques. One is reminded of the way in which modern sculptors have taken over substances such as perspex and fiberglass, and have adapted them to a new formal vocabulary which has no reference to their original use.

Solutions such as this are not, of course, the only choices available to the twentieth-century craftsman. Nor are the materials mandatory. Many content themselves with the tradition as they have inherited it, and it is the modifications of attitude, rather than the modifications of technique, which make their work seem modern. This is true of two male studio potters who are, apparently, resolutely traditional in their approach to their craft. They will not thank me for saying it, but the thing that most fascinated me about them, apart from the tranquil beauty of their work, was the degree to which they had each succeeded in constructing their own myth. It is perhaps no accident that they both work in porcelain, traditionally the most demanding, as well as the most sophisticated of ceramic materials.

Yeap Poh Chap is a Malay-born Chinese. The story of how he came to practice his present craft is perhaps the most tortuous in this book. Yeap was born in 1927 and came to England in 1948 as a law student, thus following the conventional pattern for the son of a prosperous father in Malaya or Singapore. Soon after he arrived in England he fell ill with tuberculosis and spent four years, on and off, in Swiss sanatoria. During this time his TB grew worse. The progress of the disease was eventually halted by a series of painful and hazardous operations, which involved the removal of some ribs and the collapsing of each lung in turn.

Yeap's memory of himself in those days is that he was a wilful playboy, "good for nothing," as he says cheerfully. In 1961, however, he met his beautiful Danish wife Brita. She took him to Denmark to meet her family. His own father had died, and his days of being a kind of remittance man were at an end. He wanted to find some means of staying on in Denmark, and to do this he had to have a job. His future father-in-law got him one as an assistant, doing the humblest jobs, in a small pottery near Aarhus. It was Yeap's first contact with clay.

The impression this encounter made on him was immediately decisive. In 1963, which was also the year in which he and Brita got married, he returned to England, and started to learn pottery at evening classes. He was transformed from a drifter into a man who was completely dedicated. He remembers that he lived in a tiny room in London, where the complete furnishings consisted of a bed, a sink, a portable cooker, a wheel, a kiln and a cupboard. From attendance at evening college where, he says, he was always "first in and last out," he progressed to three years at a London art college. Then he spent a further year at the Royal College of Art as a

84

"Trying to get the end product you've imagined and getting the extra bonus of what you haven't imagined"

Above: Yeap is a great cook as well as a great potter. He says both skills come from his Chinese heritage.

Opposite page: The brushes Yeap uses for painted decoration. Only part of his work is decorated in this way.

"Research Fellowship Student" — a good excuse, he says, to work there and use the college facilities. Finally, in 1968, he took the job he still has, as a teacher of pottery at St. Paul's School.

Yeap is a delightful man, but difficult to interview in any conventional sense. The reason is not unwillingness to talk: he talks exuberantly. Rather, it is that he does not want to theorize about himself. He sees what he makes — porcelain and some stoneware — as a very direct expression of a love of life which has been sharpened by his past suffering. Only half-jokingly, he puts his activity on a footing with his love of good food, of wine and whiskey. In addition to this, he thinks of his Chinese ancestry as something that gives him an intuitive feeling for ceramics. And it is true that his shapes — related to those found in classical Chinese porcelain but subtly different from them — have an instantly recognizable confidence and authority. He has sufficient confidence in his judgment of form to improve on what the throwing process gives him. Some of his shapes are further refined on a lathe.

William Mehornay is much younger than Yeap. He was born in Kansas City and first came to England in 1967. He was then with the American Air Force, and worked at an Air Force psychiatric hospital near Cambridge. One day, on a visit to Cambridge, he met a potter "and he gave me a bit of clay and that was it." Two things influenced his decision to stay in Britain rather than return to the United States. One was that, in a general sense, he found "the way of life and sense of value much more

"It's a question of achieving a certain sort of stillness. If you get still enough to realize that they are in fact there, things start to flow"

Left: William Mehornay coaxes a porcelain bowl to the degree of thinness he wants.

Above right: At home, Mehornay relaxes with his daughter.

Above: The kiln outside Mehornay's studio in Fen Ditton.

89

These pictures show the different stages in making a bowl: the clay is prepared, then thrown. Various tools are used — sponges and spatulas — but the most important tool is still the human hand. Everything depends on the sensitivity and steadiness of Mehornay's palms and finger tips.

related to my center." The second was that he had discovered a School of Meditation, with a Vedantic orientation, in London, and this seemed to offer him the kind of philosophy he thought he needed in his life. After studying for a year at a London art college he spent some time as an apprentice to Alan Caiger-Smith and has recently set up his own studio in a fenland village near Cambridge.

When I visited him there, Mehornay offered to throw some bowls, to give me an idea of how he worked. He said: "You'll notice that, if things are going right, they get thinner and thinner, more and more refined, as I go on. It's a question of achieving a certain sort of stillness. If you get still enough to realize that they are in fact there, things start to flow." He relates the way he throws to the technique of meditation he practices — a technique which "cleans the mind."

Mehornay is as essentially ceremonious as Yeap is unceremonious. When he took me back to Cambridge to lunch at his flat and meet his wife (a Scandinavian, like Mrs. Yeap), he carefully lit a candle on the table as we sat down. Perhaps rudely, I asked if this was done because they had a guest. "No," he replied, "we do it for every meal." Yet despite the contrast in personality, Yeap and Mehornay seem to me to have more in common than the kind of material they use and the type of wares they produce.

I have spoken of "myth" in connection with Yeap and Mehornay. What I mean by this is that each, to some extent, seems to stand outside himself

– to measure his life against an imagined ideal, just as he measures each pot against an imagined ideal. For each, it is clear, making pots is a healing process. But neither would be content if it were only that. The justification of what they do is the beauty of the product. But then again, each has a notion of seemliness, of the kind of life a man should live.

Enthusiasts have often touted the crafts, it seems to me rather crudely, as a panacea for social and psychological ills. Yeap and Mehornay accept the idea that their activity is to them therapeutic, a way of coming into contact with the true rhythm of the universe. But they would never claim that this alone is a reason for devoting an existence to it. The reason, rather, is the duty to exercise a skill which they happen to possess to an uncommon degree, and to add something to other men's lives, as well as their own, by doing so.

The last maker of pots that I want to talk about falls into no category. Yet I have a suspicion that Elizabeth Elton sums up many of the reasons why people are again turning to the crafts. She is a former children's nurse, and she keeps a sweetshop in Forest Road, Walthamstow, in Northeast London. Forest Road presents London in its most ordinary, most humdrum aspect, and there are not only twenty other highways like it, but hundreds of other sweetshops like the one Miss Elton keeps. The only thing that might make you think that this is not an establishment like all the rest is the fact that there are two or three shelves of pots against one wall.

Perhaps one point had better be cleared up at

91

"I said to myself: 'There must be more than this, there must be more!'"

once. Miss Elton is not an amateur potter. She is an associate member of the Craftsman Potters' Association, which is the main organization for craft potters in England. If she generally prefers to sell her pots herself, directly from her shop, it is because it gives her keen pleasure to watch people make their choice. "You can always tell which one they're going to have," she says, "by the way they pick it up. I like to see them do that — it tells you so much. And when I watch someone pick up one of my pots, something I've made, in that very special way, I feel I've given them something."

On my first visit to her, I arrived when the shop was still open. Our conversation was occasionally interrupted by the clang of the bell and by Miss Elton going out to serve somebody. For half an hour or so she locked the door so that I could take pictures of her on the wheel. She throws with strong, sure gestures, though she seems physically fragile.

At one moment she speaks of her plan to give up the shop if she is able to. "Of course, it's been my living," she says. "But that's why I took to pottery. I said to myself: 'There must be more than this, there must be more!' and that's when I started going to evening classes. On the other hand, I don't want to move away from here — to go and live in the country. I've got so many friends. You don't desert your friends."

Later, on another evening, I went to dinner with her. On a shelf above the fireplace in her sitting room is an array of work by other potters. Elizabeth Elton has gradually bought work by people she admires — a token of faith in their talent and in the ultimate importance of their activity. As I am looking at the collection, she hands me a pot about half the size of an ostrich egg and of the same shape, texture and color. "Feel it!" she commands. "Feel how silky it is!"

After the meal, at my request, she brings out her spinning wheel. We position it near the piano, whose top is scattered with pieces of music she is learning to play. But not content with pottery and music, she now wants to spin and weave, for the sheer satisfaction that these processes give her. When the wheel is set up, she unwraps a whole fleece she has just bought, and picks through it for me, showing me the various textures of wool which are to be found on the back of the same animal, and telling me what each is good for.

The only thing she is in the least evasive about is the question of how she finds time for all these activities. "I'm lucky," she declares. "I only need three hours sleep a night. I'm told it has something to do with how quickly you begin to dream once you've fallen asleep. Dreaming helps you sort out all the impressions you've taken in during the day. A doctor once told me I must dream very easily and directly."

Elizabeth Elton: behind her
sweetshop lies a fully
equipped pottery.

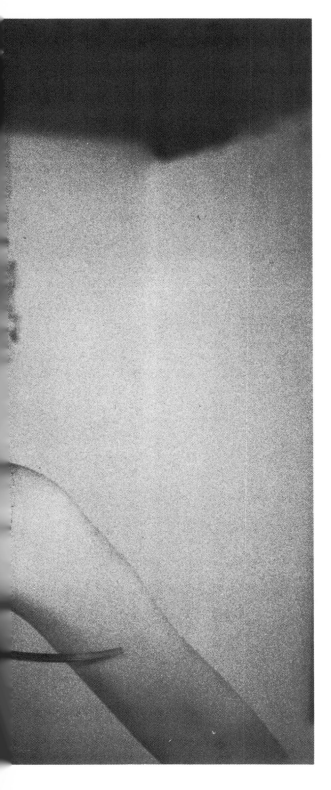

The dress-maker's dummy
which jeweler David Watkins
uses when experimenting
with his designs.

The second largest group of craftsmen whom I interviewed were the jewelers. An upsurge of interest in modern jewelry has been one of the most striking features of the general revival of interest in the crafts. A particularly interesting aspect is the relationship that exists between the modern jeweler and his patrons. The jeweler's work serves a social function, and also a psychological one. Both functions are connected with the idea of self-definition — the wearer's picture of himself or herself. If the potters tend to cast a clear light on the craftsman's relationship to his own needs, the jewelers, by contrast, are best defined in relationship to the world that surrounds them.

We live in a society which is increasingly narcissistic. We are keenly and continuously aware of our own bodies. We reshape them to fit our fantasies, not only through cosmetic surgery, but through an almost obsessive interest in diet and exercise. The wearing of jewels lends new emphasis to this physical self-awareness. Perhaps this is one among a number of reasons why it has recently become increasingly common for men to wear jewelry.

Another reason that jewels have become more important is the new candor about human sexuality. Clothes often have sexual attraction as a major part of their purpose, while their function as covering is relegated to a secondary plane. The sexual connotation of many jewels is even more emphatic than the kind of message we try to convey through our clothes.

Yet again, we live in a society which is physically increasingly mobile. One little-noticed consequence of this fact is that we have no time to enjoy our possessions. We create personal environments for ourselves which we then lack the opportunity to inhabit. Civilized men are in this sense returning to the pattern of men who are thought to be hardly civilized at all – the pattern of the nomad. The nomad's way of life requires that he always carry his possessions with him. Because the life he lives is fluid and uncertain, he also tends to think of the jewel as a talisman.

Not long ago, the jewelry made in England was arguably the most conservative in the world. Now the very opposite is true. The breakthrough happened in a number of different ways. It was, in one sense, a legacy from the so-called Swinging Sixties, part of the residue which remained after the initial excitement was over. The English were unable to sustain their position as leaders of world fashion, but certain fashion-connected activities had been liberated for good. At the same time, art in England recovered its panache and self-confidence. Even after the journalistic hubbub had died down, the world of the visual arts had a new swagger which was reflected in jewelry as well as in things like painting and sculpture. In fact, there was a tendency for jewelry to become sculpture on a small scale.

The story of how Wendy Ramshaw and her husband David Watkins came to be established as leading craft jewelers is an example of both these tendencies. They both belong, Wendy Ramshaw in particular, to the first of the two generations of experimental jewelers to have emerged in the craft world since the middle sixties.

Wendy Ramshaw was initially inspired to make jewelry through her involvement, while she was a student, with etching. She found she preferred making the plates to printing them. This tentative interest in metal and metalworking then led her to make rings, which she sold cheaply to friends. But, as she herself confesses, jewelry making was only one, and not always the most prominent, of a number of creative activities. She met her husband when he was a university art student, studying sculpture. She had been a student of illustration and fabric design, chiefly with the aim of being a teacher. David Watkins was also at that time deeply involved with the jazz scene – an involvement which eventually led him to an active participation in most areas of popular music: as a member of an R & B group, as a record producer, songwriter, and session musician.

This pop and art college background, plus the fact that Wendy was born in 1939 and David in 1940, inevitably meant that they became involved in the explosion of energy and talent that took place during the sixties. One of the things they did was to make costume jewelry, first in paper, later in plastic. In one sense, they did well. Miss Ramshaw recalls that "P.R. was there by the handful at that period." At one time they employed as many as twenty outworkers, and exported thousands of packs of paper jewelry all over the world. Once they fulfilled

Civilized men are . . . returning to the pattern of men who are thought to be hardly civilized at all — the pattern of the nomad

David Watkins does much of his work on a power-lathe.

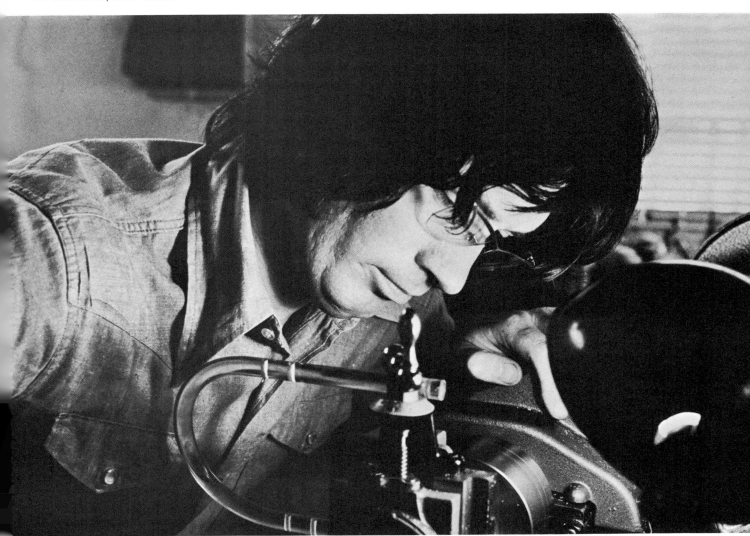

"It seemed to me that jewelry was the only creative activity in my life that had been continuous. Whatever else had happened, I'd gone on doing that. So I decided to do it properly"

Wendy Ramshaw shares a basement studio with her husband David Watkins, but they work quite separately.

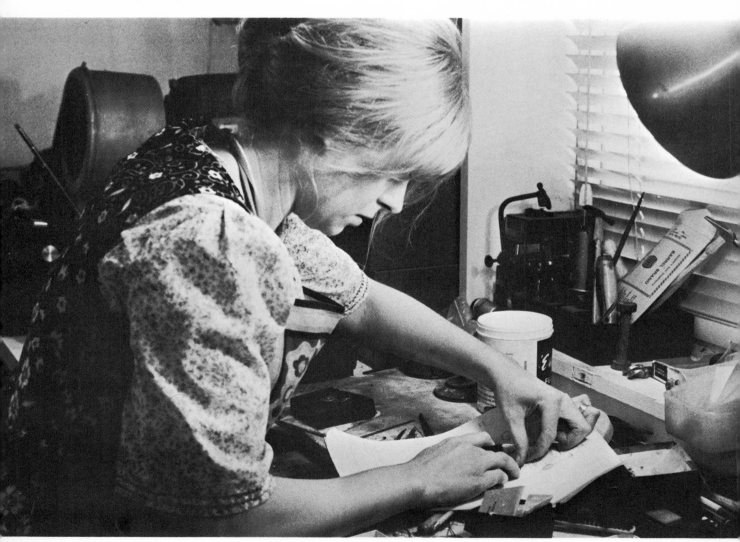

an order for 5,000 pairs of earrings in three days. The trouble was that this enormous expenditure of time, effort and energy brought only a small and uncertain financial reward. The big manufacturers copied their designs, and were much more efficient at distributing and selling the copies than Watkins and Ramshaw could hope to be with the originals, even though the originals were in fact more attractive. "It was intriguing," Wendy Ramshaw recalls, "because we got caught up with a good idea." Her husband adds, sardonically, "God protect me from good ideas."

The turning-point came when Wendy went through a period of self-questioning. "I thought," she says, "that I wasn't doing anything seriously enough. It seemed to me that jewelry was the only creative activity in my life that had been continuous. Whatever else had happened, I'd gone on doing that. So I decided to do it properly." She pauses, and adds: "I can't imagine how I thought it would be successful."

It is indicative of her coolly rational approach that she decided to concentrate on jewels whose forms sprang logically from the way a lathe works. She says: "Even before I began using a lathe I made pieces which *should*, naturally, have depended upon one." By 1966, she was already creating the multiple rings which have become a kind of Ramshaw trademark. In 1970, she felt she was ready for a one-man show.

She was determined that it must be done her way, without compromises, and when a small London gallery became interested in her work, she made it plain that she intended to keep tight control of the way in which everything was presented. Her rings were provided with specially-made stands, which turned them into parts of a small piece of sculpture when they were not in use. When the show opened, it scored a success, and marked a decisive stage in the acceptance of modern jewelry by the public.

At the time when Wendy Ramshaw's show opened, her husband David had a record in the British Top Twenty. But gradually he, too, became more and more involved with jewelry-making – first in helping Wendy to set up her workshop, then in carrying out his own ideas. Watkins's jewelry is like Ramshaw's in its clean lines, commitment to modernity and perfection of finish. His work differs from hers in style because it is bolder in scale, and shows the influence of his training as a sculptor. One gets a clear insight into his craft attitudes from the statement he provided for a recent exhibition of his work. It is worth quoting from here:

I don't have a ready-made working philosophy – only a confused and contradictory bag of tricks that under pressure I have to shuffle around. If I could possibly make things by remote control I would, which would be a pity as I actually enjoy using my skills. I have an impatience with the whole business of hand-crafting the object, and would wish it to be self-contained, a sufficiently strong expression of the few simple concepts and feelings it embodies that it needs no reference back

to the maker's hands to borrow vitality or tension. I try not to allow any current idioms or concerns of either the craft or the fashion design worlds into my work because I don't want to be pinned down by these or diverted from my own mainstream development and purpose. All the same, I hope that my work is, in broad terms, responsive to and expressive of now.

I seem to spend more time drawing and thinking and worrying about the things than actually making them, and often a whole series of ideas will result in only one piece. This is clearly wasteful as ideas which should have been realized are in some ways exorcised at the drawing board. I try not to "design" my jewelry, which may seem paradoxical but has meaning for me. Instead I try to let things fall into place and to adopt the simple, ungarnished solution if I spot it and if this sometimes gives my work an abrasive or unseductive appearance I am pleased.

He adds to this:

I don't conform to my own notion of a craftsman, let alone anyone else's, and my work is not in any way rustic or pixillated; it is serious to a degree, and in a simple way, about the ambiguous relationship of bodies and objects. I hope that my exhibition will communicate something of my feelings for these things and of my individual sense of form.

This statement of intent is much more detailed and specific than working craftsmen are usually either prepared or able to make. It illuminates some key

Above: In his London living room, David Watkins broods about the craftsman's life.

Left: David Watkins's work looks like modern sculpture. This is not surprising, since he trained as a sculptor.

issues in the craft field — the importance of deliberate experimentation, the difficulty of defining what an artist-craftsman really is, and, for that matter, what craft itself is. It becomes more illuminating still if one thinks of it in connection with the work that David Watkins is currently producing: torques and bracelets in acrylics and gold, the precise forms and subtle colors a world away from the notion of "hand finish" as Ruskin would have defined it. Even details like the way the pieces open to allow them to be put on reflect radical thinking on the part of the maker. Each hinge, on each piece, is individually designed; every catch and fastener embodies its own logic.

The basement workshop in their small London house which he shares with his wife defines their joint attitudes still further. They work amid a maze of sophisticated equipment — power-lathes and the rest. Wendy Ramshaw confesses that she is still a little frightened of some of these machines — "I know that I could easily injure myself quite badly," she remarks — but she uses them because they alone can give her what she needs to carry out her ideas. Though they do not work together on any piece, she is perhaps encouraged to go on progressing in this direction because of her husband's natural confidence with machinery. He says he can generally get any piece of equipment to produce the results he wants straight away.

At first sight, there is a striking contrast between the working surroundings that Watkins and Ramshaw have created for themselves, and those one finds in the workshop of another pair of jewelers who are almost equally well-known — Breon O'Casey and Bryan Illsley. O'Casey and Illsley work in St. Ives, where they have a small workplace in an old building which was once perhaps a fishermen's loft. Both men are painters, and they think of making jewelry as a means of supporting what they want to do in the fine arts. They use the workshop only three days a week on average, and devote the rest of the time to other occupations. O'Casey had been called away by a minor family crisis when I went to see them, and it was Illsley who talked to me and showed me around.

The equipment here is of the simplest kind. O'Casey and Illesley deliberately eschew elaborate equipment in accordance with their philosophy that materials must be handled as directly and unfussily as possible, whatever is being made. Bryan Illsley sees the closest possible connection between what he does as a jeweler and what he wants to do as a painter. Showing me some sketches for new paintings, he comments: "After all, they're as much the product of paint and paper as our jewelry is of hammers and pincers."

Illesley does not come out of the conventional art school background. His entry into this kind of activity was through a job at the Leach Pottery. As a result, he is willing to make statements which the sophisticated graduate of an art school might find naive. At one point, discussing a wooden toy he has made, and talking about its deliberate roughness and simplicity, he abruptly declares: "Of course, I think a great Romanesque head is better than

Above: Bryan Illsley in the St. Ives studio he shares with his partner Breon O'Casey.

Above right: In Illsley's narrow workshop, tools are kept in racks. A certain ordered chaos prevails.

Below left: A wooden toy made by Bryan Illsley. For him, the problems of making them are exactly the same as those involved in making jewelry.

Below right: Bryan I[
shows some of his pa[
on paper. He probably
himself first as a paint
only second as a jewe[

104

"I try to let things fall into place and to adopt the simple, ungarnished solution if I spot it"

"I hate all this fuss about the preciousness of gold. If you happen to make a jewel out of gold, that's what it happens to be made of"

Michelangelo." And then, again, fiercely: "Why does jewelry have to be so expensive, to make people think of money? I hate all this fuss about the preciousness of gold. If you happen to make a jewel out of gold, that's what it happens to be made of."

The work which O'Casey and Illsley do is in marked contrast to that produced by Ramshaw and Watkins — so much so that, as Watkins hints in the statement I have quoted, some people might be tempted to disqualify the smooth precision of his own work from the craft category at all. Yet underlying this there is, or so it seems to be, a surprising identity of circumstances. Despite the differences in approach, there is a shared belief in the absolute necessity of independence. The memory of a visit to Ramshaw and Watkins is not of the roar of their machines, but of the industriousness and happy self-enclosedness of their lives.

Wendy and David work till all hours because work is what they like to do. Wendy finds time to cook, to nurse her new son, to look after the house — and she has a daughter of school-age, too. "If I wasn't interrupted, I don't know what I'd do," she remarks. "I've got so used to interruptions." She moves among the machines in her basement for all the world like a good cook in a well-equipped kitchen. As I am about to photograph her at work, she cries, in mock horror: "Don't photograph me without my pinny! People wouldn't recognize me without my pinny!" And she dons the apron she always works in.

One comes to see that the clean lines of the jewelry she makes may, in a marginal sense at least, be seen as a kind of statement about the fullness of the life she leads, and the need to impose some kind of order upon it. In the course of our conversation I hinted at this. Wendy Ramshaw took the point, laughed, and told the story of the head of her department at a certain art school, in the days when she still taught fabric design, who could never make out how such perfect results emerged from such chaotic circumstances.

Jacqueline Mina in her tiny
workshop – a former boxroom
in a suburban house.

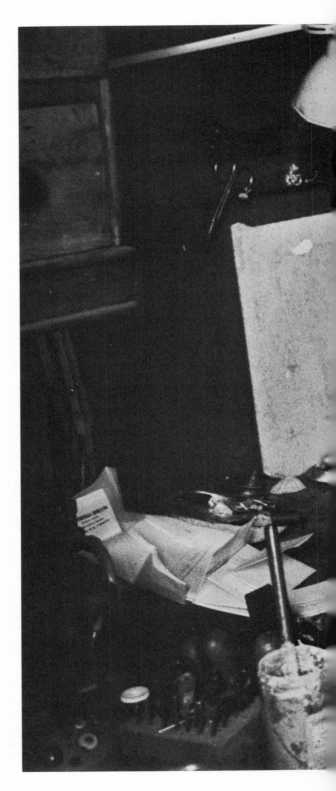

Technical ideas, and ideas about the
aesthetic of the handmade, are more closely argued
in jewelry than in any other craft activity. The
reason is that much "commercial" jewelry is also the
product of manual skills, though much trouble is
often taken to efface the marks of the craftsman's
hand. The craft jeweler is frequently uncertain
whether to reject or to imitate his uncreative
commercial rival in this respect. David Watkins and
Wendy Ramshaw stand at one end of the spectrum
of technical attitudes, Bryan Illsley and Breon
O'Casey at the other. It seems to me important to
understand that both choices have their own
validity.

Then again, the divergence about technique
cannot usefully be described in terms of personal
temperament alone. It also has something to do with
what the wearer will accept from the jewel once it
leaves the craftsman's hands. If you choose a ring
by Wendy Ramshaw, or a torque or a bracelet by
David Watkins, you are also, it seems to me,
proclaiming at least temporary allegiance to a
particular way of life: the logical commitment to the
modern which first appeared with de Stijl and
Constructivism. If you choose O'Casey's and
Illsley's work, you are probably giving evidence of
your preference for another stream of intellectual
development which is equally characteristic of our
century. For their jewels show an instinctive
understanding of, and sympathy for, the products of
ancient civilizations and primitive cultures.

The debate about techniques has been

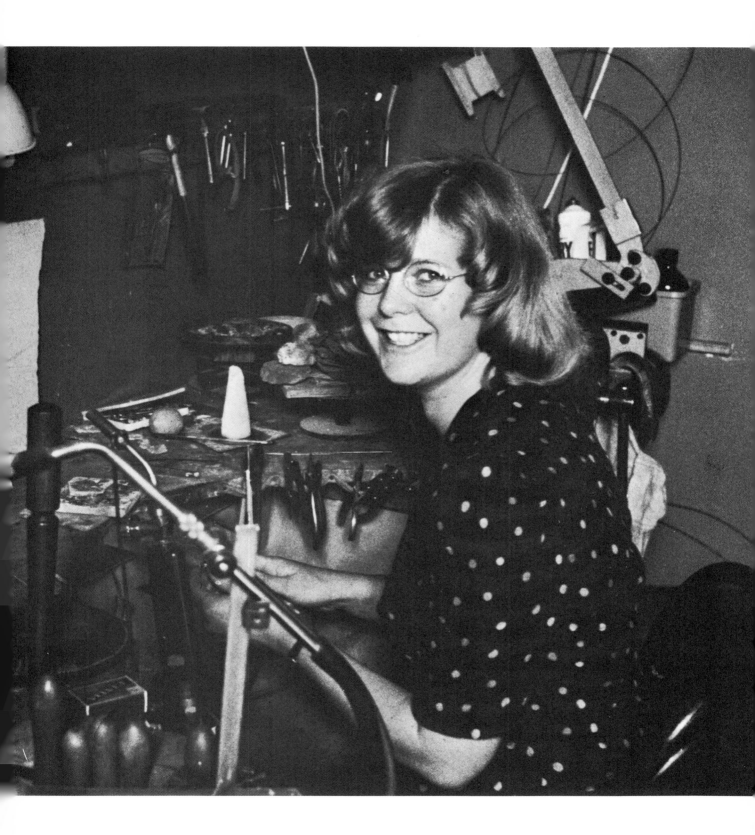

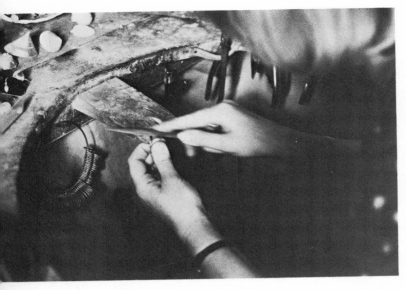

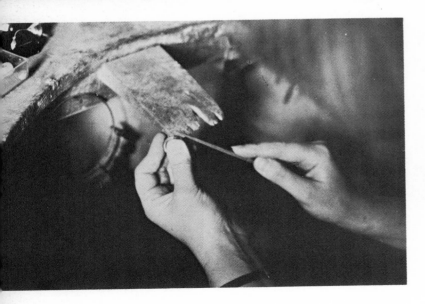

accompanied by a debate about material. Sometimes the materials used are seen as imposing their own morality — this emerges from the conversations I have already recorded. Sometimes the principle of selection can be a matter of associations. Some clients, for example, will not accept anything made from a modern synthetic substance such as acrylic, because it seems to them a betrayal of what they expect from the crafts. These are the clients who will never buy David Watkins's work. Much fiercer, however, is the argument which rages about the use of gold. The metal is a symbol for wealth insolently flaunted. It also has strong political connotations, since most of the gold available to the jeweler is mined in South Africa. For these reasons, I would go so far as to describe it as the single most controversial substance at the disposal of the modern craftsman in any field.

Jacqueline Mina is an independent woman jeweler. She works on her own in the tiny boxroom of her suburban house. She has no illusions about the economics of her profession. "Yes," she says, "of course I'm troubled by the fact that the only people who can have my work are relatively prosperous people, people who can afford it — but on the other hand I put all the money I get from my work straight into a business account, and nearly all of it goes into buying new tools and new material." She regards gold — unique in its qualities, tractable, susceptible to every variety of technical refinement — as being essential to what she wants to express.

Her family are musicians, and she feels that the

Gold — the single most controversial substance used by the modern craftman in any field

Patricia Tormey's work bench,
with stones in plastic trays.

work she does "is, in a way, like being involved with music. It's important to practice every day." As she matures, she finds her ideas about technique altering: "I'm beginning to abandon the ideas of good finish that were impressed on me at college, and to replace them with what seems a much more important factor — good construction." She adds: "Yet I'm not a designer. I'm a combiner of textures, colors and forms. And I want to reach the stage where technique is almost automatic, something very much at the back of your mind, like changing gear in a car. I want to reach the stage where I can give just one tap with the hammer, and know I've got it right, done what I wanted." But only one substance, she repeats, will allow her this freedom. "My great respect for gold and the endless variety of ways it can be worked probably influence me more than any external, existing works of art."

Patricia Tormey, like Jacqueline Mina, finds gold an essential factor in her creative expression. Tormey works mostly on commission, and she says she gets her best ideas from looking at gold and trying to form a picture of the personality of the client as it can be expressed in the metal. "Jewels are portraits," she says. "When I make one, I want it to reflect the personality of the person who is going to wear it. And gold presents its own ideas to me."

It is perhaps no accident that both of these women jewelers started out with an ambition to make sculpture. Mina says: "Right at the beginning of my first year in art school, I was asked which subject I wanted to specialize in. I would have chosen sculpture had I been a man, but though I was only sixteen at the time I was clearsighted enough to realize that if I was ever to make a mark, it would be extremely difficult, or impossible, as a sculptress." She began as a student of silversmithing and embroidery, and found that the decorative nature of the latter, combined with the techniques of the former, led her gradually to jewelry.

Tormey is bluntly amusing about the start of her vocation. "I set out to be a sculptor," she says, "realized I wasn't going to be Michelangelo, gave that up and fell in love with the metalwork master at my college of art."

Mrs. Tormey is content to react to her clients, and to use the reaction to trigger the creative process. A craftsman with a very different set of attitudes, both toward his materials and toward the people who will wear what he makes, is David Poston. For reasons of political conviction, Poston uses neither gold nor diamonds in his work. It is his form of protest against the attitudes of the South African government. He, more than most craftsmen, is aware of the dilemma of the man who works for a luxury market, and who yet wants his product to be an integral part of a way of life directed against luxury — a rejection of the bourgeois society for which jewels are usually made.

The setting in which Poston works is so much a part of his philosophy that it needs to be described. It is an unusual place for a jeweler to choose to live. Not that Poston himself is anyone's idea of what such a person should look like. He is a burly

"Jewels are portraits. When I make one, I want it to reflect the personality of the person who is going to wear it. And gold presents its own ideas to me"

six-footer, diffident and exuberant by turns, expansive then intense. He is now in his mid-twenties, and he has recently gone back to live on the Isle of Portland, where he spent part of his adolescence.

Portland is to all intents and purposes a real island, but is tenuously joined to the southern coast of England by Chesil Beach. Thomas Hardy described it as stretching out "like the head of a bird" into the English Channel. Hardy also spoke of the "strange beliefs and singular customs" that once prevailed there. The island is famous for its quarries – Wren's St. Paul's is faced with Portland stone. The quarries brought the convicts, who were imported to work the mines in the nineteenth century. Since the early middle ages, the island has been a point of military defense. Quarries, convicts and military installations still bring Portland its livelihood.

David Poston is not a born Portlander. He was born in 1948 in Moscow, where his father was in the British diplomatic service. The family came to Portland when Poston's father retired. He joined the Church of England and was appointed chaplain to the prison on the island.

The road back to Portland, for Poston himself, has been a complicated one. He went to a famous public school and hated it. Later he went to Hornsey College of Art. Here he attended the jewelry design course, but the thing that influenced him most had nothing to do with the curriculum he was supposed to pursue. It was a period of great student unrest, especially in art schools. The unrest culminated in

Opposite page, above: The room where Tormey works. A cork panel above the bench is for pictures which either amuse or inspire her.

Opposite page, below: Tormey uses a lot of baroque pearls. She increases her stock of them whenever she can.

Above: The hat is a Tormey trademark. She wears it even when she is working.

Jeweler David Poston. Behind him are the spectacular cliffs of the Isle of Portland, where he lives.

what since has become legendary as "the Hornsey sit-in." Poston took an extremely active part in this, though he resists suggestions that he was one of the leaders. "The essence was that there *was* no leader." He now describes the experience as being "very highly educational in the best sense — a matter of examining things and questioning them very hard." During his last year, he was one of the first two student governors at Hornsey.

Jewelry has by no means occupied all his life since he left art school. He earned his living as a photographer, as a truck driver, and by doing whatever else turned up — without ever quite ceasing to make jewels. Early in 1972 he went to Stockholm to do a photographic documentation of a mime course. Later still he was props master at the local theater in Newcastle. When I expressed slight surprise at this choice of occupation, he replied: "Where could I possibly have got a job that involved making more things, and more different things, than the one I had? The only trouble was that you never got time to solve your problem. You always had to fudge it."

Dissatisfaction with the conditions under which he was working in the theater led him to return to London and start making jewelry full time again. What he did began to attract attention, but he decided that he couldn't continue to live in the metropolis. Portland drew him: he already had a boat there, and all his life he has had a passion for the sea. So he looked for a place to live in Fortuneswell, the steep, grey little town that

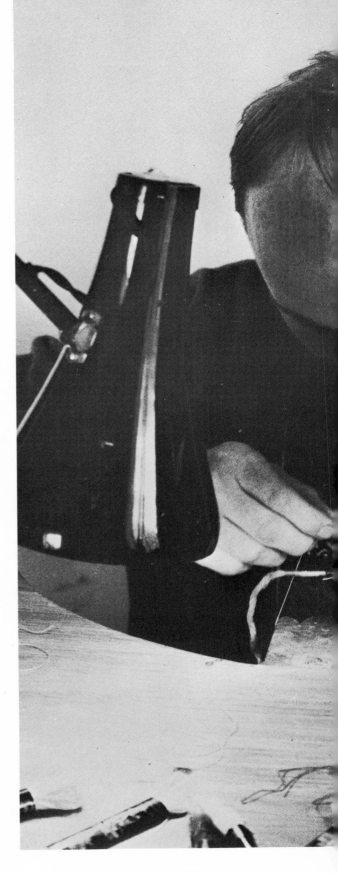

overlooks the Chesil Beach.

David Poston has recently been described as the most interesting radical craftsman in England, but one feels a little uncertain about the way the adjective is meant to be taken, or, indeed, whether Poston would accept its implications himself. He is radical in politics, certainly — his refusal to make jewelry in gold is consistent with his whole philosophy. Not only does this refusal shut him out of the wealthier end of the market, but he feels it as a real creative deprivation. He, too, is fascinated by the sensuous qualities of fine gold, and its unique tractability in the craftsman's hands.

Yet he could also be described as radical in his attitudes to materials. Much of his recent work has been made with things such as hemp and colored embroidery cotton. Handmade beads in silver and azurite will be interspersed with Turk's Head knots. Or a large bead made of carved slate will slide on a multi-colored circlet made of whipped embroidery cotton on black plastic-covered nylon thread. His techniques derive not only from his training as a jeweler but from his experience of the sea and of sailing, just as he occasionally makes use of pebbles picked up on Chesil Beach. Many of these methods take inordinate amounts of time and patience, and he seems to find a satisfaction in them for this very reason. He remarked to me at one point that much of what he did was "more in the nature of therapy" than of "being creative."

Much of what Poston does is intended to be therapeutic for the wearer as well. He thinks that

120

"Jewelry is a means of reconciling people to their bodies, making them feel switched on. It is about how they feel inside and how they can realize that feeling"

Right: Poston uses a lot of hemp in his work. He is an expert in nautical skills, as well as in the jeweler's craft.

Above: Here Poston works on a silver buckle which has just been cast. The mold was made from a boxwood model he carved.

"jewelry is a means of reconciling people to their bodies, making them feel switched on. It is about how they feel inside and how they can realize that feeling." Inviting me to handle a piece he was working on, he commented: "My principal language is touch."

Poston seems very different in attitudes from David Courts and William Hackett. He lives almost as a recluse, while they inhabit a gregarious society with strong show-business connections. Yet it is typical of the paradoxical nature of the modern craft scene that it was Poston who sent me to see them. Courts was a contemporary of Poston's at Hornsey. Later, he attended the Royal College of Art, where he met his present partner. When I met them, they were busy setting up a new workshop in London.

In the little world of craft-jewelers, certain pieces rapidly acquire a legendary reputation. Craftsman after craftsman will ask you if you have seen a particular object, made by some friend or rival. David Courts is the maker of a necklace which has gathered around itself a legend of this kind. The central motif represents a phoenix, made of gold touched with enamel, and holding a small amethyst in its claws. The openwork wings are arranged to open stage by stage, like the blades of a fan – but first one must release a hidden catch. The finish of the piece is arrogantly perfect; it is a virtuoso demonstration of the metalworker's art.

Hackett is a craftsman of the same order of technical accomplishment. He has a necklace of his own to set beside Courts's phoenix. The centerpiece

"My principal language is touch"

Right: William Hackett (left) and David Courts (right) in their Hampstead workshop.

Above: Two spectacular jewels. The one on the left is by Hackett, the one on the right by Courts.

123

Above: Hackett points proudly to the gold and silver fly he made. It is mounted on a long pin.

Opposite page: Gold and silver studio: modern jewelery in the very heart of Georgian Bath.

represents a kind of beetle whose body, under the golden wing-cases, consists of a fine opal, half-concealed. He also shows me a second example of his skill – a fly in gold and oxidized silver, mounted on a pin. Fingering this piece, he remarks: "I don't think I could ever sell it. When you've put as much into a piece as I have into this one, you don't want to part with it. All my girl friends try to get it out of me. Sometimes I wear it to parties, like this…" And he thrusts the pin into his red waistcoat until it vanishes, leaving the metal fly perched on the cloth. "Of course, I always go in these clothes, because these are what I've got."

Courts and Hackett are in striking opposition to most of the other jewelers I interviewed – except, perhaps, Watkins and Ramshaw – in their indifference to the notion of the personal touch. To them, perfection of finish is infinitely more important, which is why they envisage that they will work together on the same piece. This indifference is also the reason that they are perfectly prepared to have a particular component made up outside, if they think it will be better executed than they will do it themselves.

It is as if the world they belong to – a world of young and beautiful actresses, of rock stars with Rolls Royces – has a need of its own court goldsmiths, its own Cellinis, ready to make things of extravagant beauty to match a wild and extravagant way of life. This is the role they are preparing to fulfil. But not cynically.

Their contempt for the individual thumbprint is

124

"If you were working on your own, you might get frightened, think the client wouldn't like it, think you couldn't do it, not push things far enough. But a partner won't let you do that —he'll egg you on"

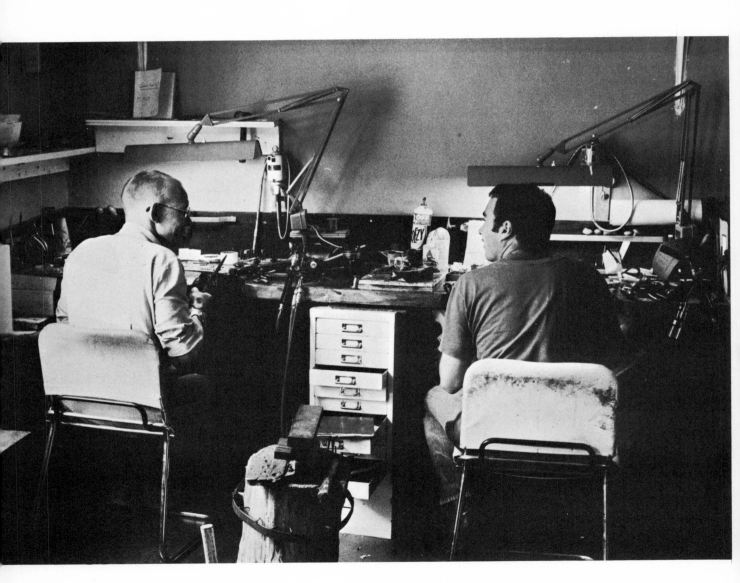

matched by their genuine respect for virtuosity as
something that can be objectively judged. David
Courts, for example, talks of the advantages of
working in partnership with someone whose skill
and imagination you respect: "If you were working
on your own, you might get frightened, think the
client wouldn't like it, think you couldn't do it, not
push things far enough. But a partner won't let you
do that — he'll egg you on." Hackett describes
himself as having been basically uninterested, until
recently, in the final result: "Making things didn't
interest me much. Mastering techniques did." He,
like Poston, has no respect for those who fudge it.

Courts and Hackett have another link with
Poston as well, and perhaps this link also binds them
to jewelers like Tormey and Mina. None of them is
content to produce mere ornaments — they all want
to make objects which are certainly talismanic and
possibly therapeutic. The precise nature of their
effort emerged when Hackett was searching for a
phrase which would embody the effect which he and
Courts want their work to produce. Virtuosity, for
him, leads beyond mere perfection to a kind of
indefinable *frisson*: "I think of the things I want to
make as being what I call 'little magics.' "

It seems to me that there are also links between
Courts and Hackett and Trevor Marsh and David
Tucker, two young jewelers who now work in
partnership in the golden Georgian city of Bath. The
latter, however, have emerged from a very different
background; and their work, too, is strikingly
dissimilar from that which Courts and Hackett

Above: David Tucker works on a tricky bit of soldering.

Opposite page: Malcolm Appleby shapes an iron bracelet blank on an anvil.

Overleaf: Further work on the same bracelet blank. Appleby's workshop is an abandoned railway station.

produce. Marsh and Tucker no longer worship virtuosity — perhaps because they have too close and intimate an experience of it.

They are boyhood friends who went to art school together. After a brief training they both spent a five-year apprenticeship in Hatton Garden, the center of the English commercial jewelry industry, working for a firm of diamond mounters — by all accounts, a fairly rigorous form of servitude. Later, they enlarged their experience by working for successful firms on the borderline between "high fashion" and craft jewelery. They finally decided to set up an independent partnership, and chose Bath as a pleasant place in which to base themselves.

The jewelry they now make may come as something of a shock if one knows about their background. It is as fierce and barbarous as that of Watkins and Ramshaw is sleek and cool. Instead of acrylic and enamel, they offer combinations of leather and mammoth ivory, blackened iron and hammered silver. It's almost as if their long Hatton Garden apprenticeship had called for a deliberate revolt against the blind respect for precision for precision's sake. Yet to see them at work is to notice that old skills die hard. I watched Marsh making the collets needed to set a group of stones in a piece he had on the bench. The task was done with a speed, a confidence and a skill which his old colleagues would surely have approved. However, the outer man, so he tells me, would be someone whom these same colleagues would scarcely recognize. "In London I always wore suits," he says, "but now I

"I think of the things I want to make as being what I call 'little magics'"

don't own one." On his wrist is a superb bracelet of his own making, in silver and gold. It shows a Valkyrie with a carved, golden face and gold-striped shield. It is studded with a boss of malachite and lined with leather. He echoes Hackett when I ask him about it: "Sometimes you make things which you think are too good to sell."

One of the things that fascinate me most about the Marsh-Tucker partnership is the question of whom they sell to. Their work seems so completely at odds with the elegant Georgian architecture of their surroundings. "Young people, I think," Tucker says. Marsh chimes in: "We sell to people like us, who come from another part of the country. People who've chosen to live here, and who've fulfilled themselves by doing their own particular thing, just as we have, which they wouldn't have done if they'd stayed where they were. What I like about the people who buy from us is that they've got a certain sincerity. They've made up their minds that they *want* something of ours." And his final comment on the situation is: "We both used to be very sophisticated. Now we're very unsophisticated. The work itself has brought about that situation, and very dramatically."

Marsh and Tucker see themselves as having embarked on a voyage of self-discovery, in collaboration with the people who buy their work. But one cannot pretend that the relationship between the avant-garde jeweler and his clientele is always idyllic. I am not speaking here of trivialities such as the behavior of the occasional individual client who

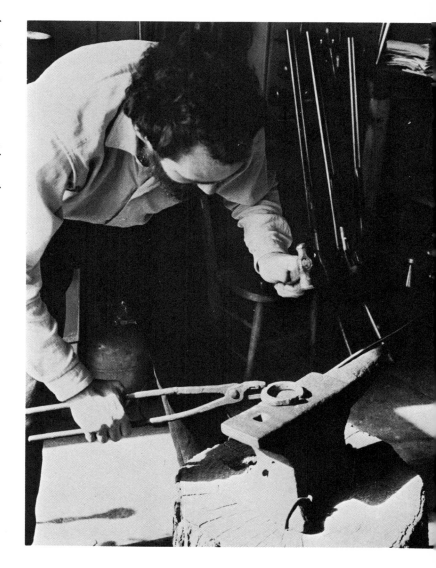

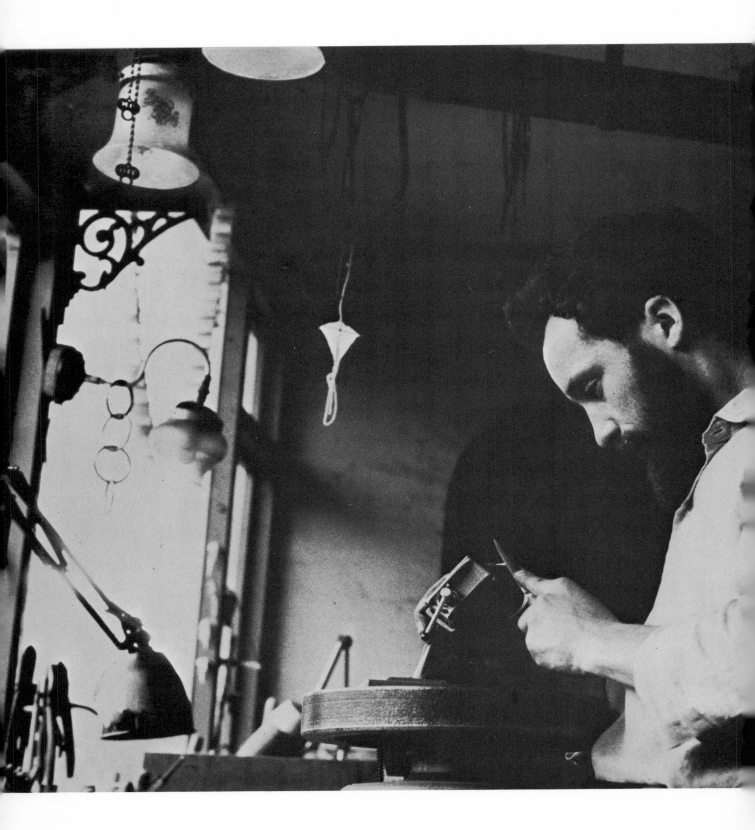

"What I like about the people who buy from us is that they've got a certain sincerity. They've made up their minds that they want something of ours"

determines on occasion to satisfy his or her own caprices. It is simply that there was no unanimity among the jewelers I interviewed on the subject of client relationships, and particularly on the vexed subject of working on direct commission. Some, such as Tormey, find it stimulating and feel that contact with the eventual wearer is an integral part of the creative process. Others find it difficult to accommodate their own ideas to the buyer's demands.

There is undoubtedly a mystique that surrounds the jewel, and it is difficult to be certain if this is linked with, or opposed to, its organic connection with the world of fashion and money. Most of the jewelers I spoke to are fascinated with the idea that, for the maker, the jewel can embody ideas and feelings almost as a poem can. On the other hand, they recognize that the jewel is an instrument of self-recognition for the person who wears it.

And most of them are, at least in some degree, made uncomfortable by the intrinsic value of the materials. The use of such materials seems to bind them inexorably to a way of life and a view of society which they are struggling to escape. Poston, the most uncompromising in his revolt against bourgeois standards, has the keenest awareness of the dilemmas imposed on him by his chosen activity, but he is not the only one to suffer from them.

Of all the jewelers I interviewed, only one seems to have found a solution completely satisfactory to himself. This was Malcolm Appleby, who is perhaps better described as a master metalsmith, than as a

Overleaf: In Malcolm
Appleby's workshop some
neighbors have dropped by for
a friendly chat.

"I like to do things which the people who live round here can afford, and which I can afford to do for them in terms of time and effort"

jeweler proper.

Appleby lives in an abandoned railway station, some fourteen or fifteen miles outside Aberdeen, Scotland. He is not a Scotsman by birth, but comes from Beckenham in Kent, almost at the other end of the British Isles, where his father is a parking lot attendant. He and Poston belong to the same generation – Appleby was born in 1948, and is thus eight years younger than David Watkins.

Appleby and his way of life are something of a legend in craft circles. He has been the subject of a number of recent articles, most of them very romantic in tone, and he has also been the hero of a television film. Appleby himself dismisses most of this publicity, with a derisive snort, as "fairy tales." The reality, as I discovered, corresponds to the legend in one sense and belies it in another.

Crathes station is a long low building, with a little wood behind it. Appleby works, and mostly lives, in the largest space, which must be the old waiting room. There is a small stove in the middle and a vast old mirror at one end. The floor is bare concrete, and there is an anvil, and benches crowded with equipment. The only sign of conversion or renovation is the big window that fills one side of the room. Hens wander up and down the disused platform outside, and occasionally stray into the workshop.

Appleby has a gift for making one feel that one has just stepped into a perfectly natural and continuing situation. Almost as soon as he'd greeted me, he was back at work – on a model for a medal depicting Edinburgh Castle. A little later his friend Jenny Watson arrived. With Mrs. Watson was her mother. Conversation flowed, I made some photographs, and Appleby got on with the job. Every now and then a hen would stray in and take a slightly disapproving look at us.

An hour or so later we broke for coffee, and Mrs. Watson drove us the mile or so to Crathes Castle. Crathes Castle is the property of the National Trust for Scotland, and here, in the canteen, we sat ourselves down and looked at snapshots of a local wedding. There was much backchat and laughter, with the waitresses delightedly reproving Appleby for being "dreadful." While we sat there he got out a hank of wool and a darning needle, and started mending the front of his extremely disreputable sweater – a totem object, as I afterwards discovered. A group of tourists watched him goggle-eyed.

Back at the station, he began to talk of his arrival at Crathes – a house, rented on impulse from friends, had led to his purchase of the building he now has. He described with relish his forays as a junk-collector. A 'thirties Meccano set, still in its original box and found by the wreckers in a house that was being demolished, had been cannily swapped for the hens and their coop. A toy farm from the same source had fetched top price when he gave it to a local charity auction. Appleby says: "Do you know, I thought when I came here I'd never see anyone. In fact, I often see as many as fifteen people a day. But the locals are very tactful – they drop in,

132

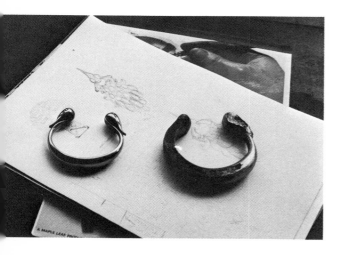

Left: A finished bracelet in gold and iron (left) and the way a similar bracelet looks when Appleby has just begun work on it.

Center: Crathes Railway Station. Grass grows on the tracks, and the waiting room has become the main work space.

Bottom: Medals designed by Malcolm Appleby. It requires enormous skill to cut the dies.

say hullo, and let you get on with it."

Appleby is a little reluctant to talk about his work — at least, about the reasons for it. He is more loquacious about the way he became a professional craftsman. It arose, he says, from his interest in guns. This led him to engraving, and then to an apprenticeship with a gun engraver. Gun engravers were in short supply when he began — he had the luck, he says, to learn the skill while actually doing the job.

Since then he has gone on to establish himself as Britain's most celebrated engraver in metal. It was he, for example, who did the engraving for the coronet which was used when Prince Charles was formally invested with his title as Prince of Wales at Caernarvon. He makes jewelry in precious metals and in steel damascened with gold, and he engraves dies for medals. For some years he has been engaged in making a superb chess set, one piece at a time. It is in steel inlaid with gold and silver, finely engraved and chased. Each of the chessmen has his own individuality. And Appleby still keeps his hand in as a gun engraver.

Some of his work is done for people who live locally — a wedding ring, engraved as he said "with the weather," for a neighbor about to get married; a silver bracelet with gunsmith scrolls for Jenny Watson's mother. "I like to do things which the people who live round here can afford, and which I can afford to do for them in terms of time and effort," he remarks. "Sometimes it's difficult to get people to see why a steel bracelet inlaid with gold

"I prefer things to be a bit of a challenge. I think of something, and I want to find out if it can be done — if I can do it"

costs more than a silver one – though it's harder to make and takes much longer." The rest of the time, Appleby works on commissions from London and elsewhere. Some, like the chess set, will take him years to complete.

"Sometimes," he remarks, "you don't know what you're taking on." He produces a ring in steel and gold in the form of a hawk's head. "When I made this, I didn't know what I was letting myself in for. It all had to be carved out of the solid metal. I keep it here because I don't know if I'll ever do another one like it." It lives on his workbench in a little earthenware box. The box was specially designed as a foil to the splendor concealed within it.

It is now late afternoon, and Appleby has changed tasks. He is hammering and filing the blank for a steel bracelet. "Though I've made one or two of these," he says, "I don't mind making another one, as I think there is still something to be found out concerning this particular job. I prefer things to be a bit of a challenge. I think of something, and I want to find out if it can be done – if *I* can do it." Idly, I ask him how many hours he works. "Oh, most days till nine or ten at night."

In the early evening, the local taxi-service comes to pick me up and return me to Aberdeen. The driver leaves me in no doubt that I have been received by a local celebrity. For some reason I recall Appleby's remark over lunch – a casserole of stewed grouse and pigeon. "It's all meat," he says, as we pick at the bones. "I only like things which are really nourishment."

In a world which seems increasingly hostile to any taint of the "literary" in the visual arts, it may at first come as a surprise to find a large number of craftsmen devoting themselves to the arts of the book. In addition to this, there is the fact that we tend to think of books as being entirely functional objects. The beauty of Keats's poetry is in no way affected if we read him in paperback. And if we happen to dog-ear the pages, or to mark our place with the butter knife, the quality of the text itself is never affected.

Yet there is a continuous tradition in the production of fine books which goes back many centuries beyond the Arts and Crafts Movement. It was already old when the Lindisfarne Gospels were produced. Nevertheless, the craftsmen of the late nineteenth century were particularly interested in this sphere of activity, perhaps because it promised a direct link between the labor of the hand and the work of the mind. Fine books were among the most characteristic products of the craftsmen of the time, and what is being done today can be traced directly to these predecessors. The books that Morris himself issued from his Kelmscott Press are now universally recognized as being perhaps his finest decorative achievement. Kelmscott in turn inspired a number of worthy successors — Ashbee's Essex House Press, Charles Ricketts's Vale Press, Lucien Pissarro's Eragny Press, and the Doves Press of T. J. Cobden-Sanderson and Emery Walker. Fine printing also begat fine binding. The finest bindings of all were probably those produced at the Doves

Above: Will Carter (left) and his son Sebastian (right) sit on an upturned punt in the garden of their house by the river Cam.

Above, right: In the background of this picture is the handsome old house that is the headquarters of the Rampant Lions Press.

Below, right: The basement workshop where Will and Sebastian Carter produce their books.

139

"Working single-handed, with what must of necessity be a limited range of types, teaches one quicker than anything not to embark on elaborate settings, or anything which is at all complicated when it need not be so"

Bindery.

When the main Arts and Crafts tradition faltered, the effort to produce fine books – books which were a sensuous pleasure to look at and to handle – continued with remarkable vigor. A firm of London binders, Messrs. Sangorski & Sutcliffe, to take one example, was founded in 1901 and is still in business in premises it has occupied since 1912. It has triumphantly survived two World Wars and the intervening slump.

Representative of the continuous tradition of fine printing that can be traced back to Kelmscott is the Rampant Lions Press of Will and Sebastian Carter. They are a father-and-son team, who work from the basement of a fine house in Cambridge. Though they enjoy an enviable reputation as printers – in 1971 the Grolier Club of New York initiated a series of exhibitions of the work of contemporary fine printers with a display from the Rampant Lions Press – they are perhaps more modest and certainly more thoroughly practical in their aims than Morris and his immediate successors.

Their claim is: "We design everything we print, but we do not print everything we design." Their work covers an immense range. There are books under their own and other imprints, but this is only the tip of the iceberg. They produce paper bags, college guides, reports and accounts, tickets, lettered book jackets, all kinds of stationery, menus and programs, legal documents and book labels.

Nor does printing constitute the whole of their activity. They also cut lettering in stone and wood, design inscriptions for cutting in metal, and make designs for shopfronts and directional signs. Will Carter says of the jobbing work they undertake that "it has the advantages for a designer-printer of ensuring a constant flow of design problems of inexhaustible variety, which keeps him constantly on his aesthetic toes." He describes the Press, which he founded in 1948, as a way of "achieving any kind of life where one could do what one wanted, even if one had no money at all."

In one sense, the comparison with Morris remains inescapable. One recent project undertaken by the Carters shows how direct it can be. A new publication from their workshop not only contains a text by Morris – "The Story of Cupid and Psyche" from his collection of verse-tales *The Earthly Paradise* – but is set in Morris's own "Troy" type, specially recast from the original matrices (molds). This book is designed to serve as a framework for a series of woodblock illustrations which were drawn by Burne-Jones and mostly engraved on the wood by Morris himself, but which had remained unused until now.

In another sense, however, "The Story of Cupid and Psyche" illustrates the difference between the Kelmscott philosophy and that of the Rampant Lions Press. The Carters have no house style as such – the format adopted for a particular job is the format that seems appropriate to the task in hand. "Troy" was chosen for the book I have just described because that was the type that seemed to complement the illustrations best. The huge variety

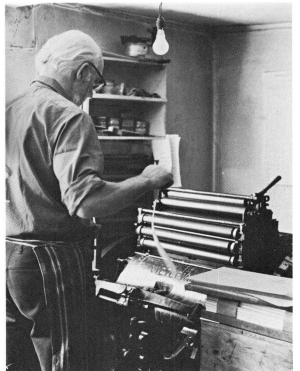

Above: Will Carter checks the alignment of a page. It doesn't matter that the type is upside down.

Left: Will Carter at work on a press.

141

"One becomes very conscious of the tricks played by the eye, which can be anticipated during the actual setting of the job, before proofing."

of jobs undertaken in the Carter workshop contrasts with the rarefied atmosphere of Morris's enterprise, where the press concentrated quite simply on producing the finest possible books, virtuoso demonstrations of the skills of designer, typographer and printer.

One must not, however, try to minimize Will Carter's commitment to the job. He has been fascinated by printing ever since, as a boy of twelve, he paid a visit to the Clarendon Press in Oxford. He soon owned a small Adana flat-bed press, and when he left school the jobs he took were nearly all concerned with publishing and printing. What led him to set up on his own was a theory "that there was a market for fine jobbing printing of the sort that was too small to be handled by the big printing houses and yet was beyond the scope of the small jobbing house." He tested this theory, found it worked, and enthusiasm and economic survival were thus brought into a workable relationship with one another.

The outstanding quality of the work done at the Rampant Lions Press is its straightforwardness. In a written account, published to celebrate the first ten years of the enterprise, Will Carter has this to say: "Working single-handed, with what must of necessity be a limited range of types, teaches one quicker than anything not to embark on elaborate settings, or anything, in fact, which is at all complicated when it need not be so. One soon develops a house style – not of the kind usually meant by that term, but a style of design and

Above: Sebastian Carter collates the pages of an unbound book.

Opposite page: Will Carter is also well known as a cutter of inscriptions. He feels this type of work sharpens his eye for the balance of type on a page.

presentation which becomes easily recognizable by those interested in such matters. I fancy that mine is the frequent use of large italics, often printed in gray to disguise their size, and a partiality for Bembo."

He adds: "The setting out of lettering for incised inscriptions on stone taught me to have a very sharp eye for points of spacing — letter spacing, word spacing and interlinear spacing — and this has been put to good use. It means that one becomes very conscious of the tricks played by the eye, which can be anticipated during the actual setting of the job, before proofing. It is these points that make all the difference between a good and an ordinary piece of printing, though you might be hard put to it to say just why. I have found that the concentration of designer, compositor and pressman in one person is the best if not the *only* way that small jobs can be done properly — and done quickly, for economics count for a great deal in a shop like mine."

Now that Will Carter has been joined at the Rampant Lions Press by his son Sebastian, they preserve this sensitivity to the look of the page by dividing the jobs between them, so that each has responsibility for a particular commission, and follows it through from start to finish.

The development of the Press has led, inevitably, to some changes in emphasis. As its reputation grew, there were more and more commissions for bookwork; and this in turn led to a decision to run down the jobbing side, though not to abandon it.

An important point, for those interested in the craftsman and his situation, is the way Will Carter,

"The creative bookbinder...tries to express and interpret the total literary thematic concept of the book"

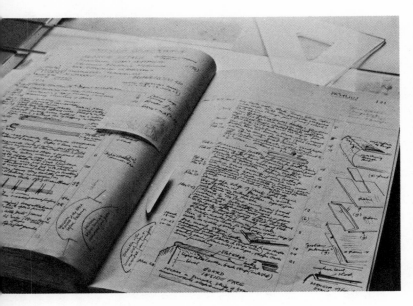

Above: All experiments and variations in technique are carefully recorded in Philip Smith's big notebook.

Opposite page: Philip Smith builds up a pictorial design from innumerable small pieces of leather and from scraps of 'Maril,' a leather compound with random streaks and splashes of color which he invented himself.

like Eric Gill before him, has been able to feed the specifically craft experience back into the industrial situation by designing typefaces for general use. This is unlike Morris's attitude, for Morris knew that his typefaces were only suitable for the kind of job that Kelmscott did. Carter, on the other hand, looks outside his own situation as a craftsman-printer. The best known of his typefaces is Klang, issued in 1955 as Monotype Series 593. This later developed into Klang Bold. Klang has its roots in Carter's experience of pen-drawn lettering, so in this case the wheel has indeed come full-circle.

Leading contemporary bookbinders, such as Philip Smith, Faith Shannon or Trevor Jones, pursue rather a different line. Philip Smith, an outstanding craftsman who is also particularly articulate about his aims is a case in point. Smith sees bookbinding as "a recently reevaluated and as yet unrecognized medium of expression," very much on a footing with painting, sculpture, and even with film-making. "The creative bookbinder," he says, "is working with a parallel but different medium. With an objective inner eye he tries to express and interpret the total literary thematic concept of the book. Instead of insight into the nature of a landscape or a person or some abstract concept of color, space or time, the binder has the (sometimes) carefully chosen literary work as his springboard to insight and expression."

What Smith means by this can be seen in the work he has recently undertaken. Even by the standards of the great bookbinders of the past, some of this is exceptionally ambitious. He has, for

example, made a whole series of bindings for J. R. Tolkein's epic narrative *The Lord of the Rings*. It was his intention, he says:

> to communicate the emotional flavors which can be strongly felt running through the epic. This does not mean a duplication of the inside on the outside of the book, but a visual summing-up of the main themes, tempered naturally by my own subjective view. I have at the same time attempted a kind of imagery which allows of free interpretation on the part of the spectator who has read the book... Many of the separate images are 'open-ended' and may be contemplated much as one might muse about 'pictures in the fire' or the image on the face of the moon. Laced throughout are more concrete images providing a toe hold for the imaginative faculty.

What Smith has done is to create what he dubs a "book wall" composed of twenty-one book covers. Each of the three volumes of the work has been bound several times over — the upper row of the wall consists of seven copies of volume one, the middle row of seven copies of volume two, the third and lowest of seven copies of volume three. The books are displayed within a specially-constructed framework. Each binding is complete in itself, but the whole is greater than the sum of the individual parts. The binder remarks that "throughout the epic story there are a series of dynamic movements (the single covers) and only at the end of the adventure is rest implied."

Obviously a project of this sort takes the

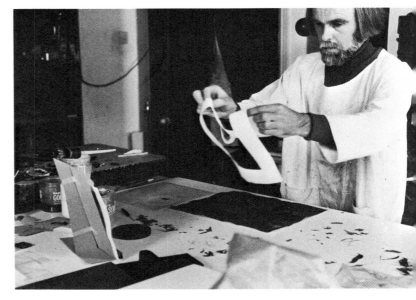

"If one is to continue the elusive and not quite attainable goal of creating something really 'whole,' one has to build a set up and system making the activity practical and economically viable"

binder's function into an entirely new realm. And this conceptual breakthrough is matched by the elaboration and the refinement of Smith's technique. Basically, what he works with is leather. Leather onlays are used to make an elaborate pictorial pattern, which is further elaborated with smaller fragments of leather and with slivers of a substance, which Smith is responsible for inventing, called "Maril." Maril is a marbled material made by compressing scraps and shavings of different colored leathers, the waste products of the binder's workshop, into a solid block. The block can again be shaved to produce strips and slivers which are full of suggestive random patterns. Smith points out that he can get a refinement of detail with this which he could not obtain (even if he had unlimited time at his disposal) by placing and fixing minute fragments of a single color. Even so, he will spend up to 600 working hours on the creation of a single binding, and an important example of his skill will cost the client at least as much as a good modern painting.

The practical function of the binding, as a protection for the leaves of paper it encloses, tends to take second place to the expressive function of what is done. Yet Smith agrees that "the binding cannot be divorced from the total being of the book, its structure and physical appearance." He thinks that the leather panel differs fundamentally from the covering of a book not only because the latter is, as he puts it, "a mobile variable solid." He continues: "The text provides two further dimensions: the dimension of time (it requires duration to read a

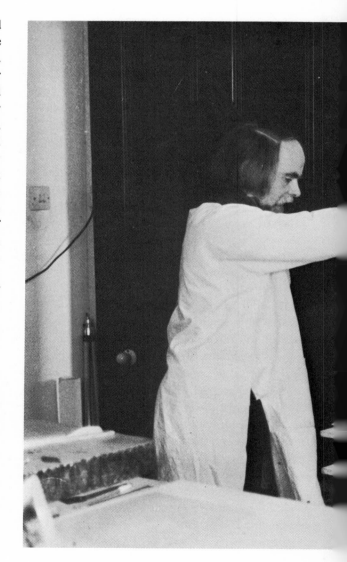

148

Left: Philip Smith puts a book in the press, one of the most traditional and essential pieces of bookbinder's equipment.

Above: A binding must work three-dimensionally, not just as a flat surface. Here Smith checks to see that it does.

149

Above: Faith Shannon in her bindery.

Opposite page: Faith Shannon is an inveterate collector. Her living room shows a throng of objects. Many are examples of 'popular' art.

sequence of word images), and the dimension of ideas, thoughts and emotions. The design of the covers provides an overall dimension by the summing up of this duration period or flow of ideas in one open-ended image, creating an expansion of the present moment."

Much of this may seem to be in sharp contrast to Will Carter's attitudes. Yet there are some areas of agreement as well. In a letter to me, written after I had been to see him at work, Smith wrote:

On looking back I don't think we discussed "reasons" why one occupies oneself at this form of activity (bookbinding) in the late twentieth century. Apart from the questionable issue as to whether one can control one's life or have any real choice in the matter, there is some inner compulsion which drives one down a particular avenue (suited to one's potentials) strive as one might to move in other directions. But then one begins to see that one can attain what one is after and one loves what one sees is being done. Then of course if one is to continue the elusive and not quite attainable goal of creating something really "whole," one has to build a set up and system making the activity practical and economically viable. That is not quite the story of my life, but it might help!

Because he is able to treat binding as a full-time activity, Smith differs from the other two bookbinders I interviewed. But they, too, are people who treat binding not merely as a means of clothing a book, but also as a way of creating what amounts

to an independent work of art.

Faith Shannon was born in 1938 in India, where her father, an army officer, was then serving. She is, as her name would suggest, of Irish descent; she spent her childhood in Northern Ireland. Like many women who find their means of expression in the crafts, she started off by wanting to be a fine artist — in her case, a painter. When she began her studies at the Belfast College of Art, she was told that she had to take a subsidiary subject in addition to her course in painting. Since the sculpture class was full, and since she had always been good at handling paper, and making things with it, she chose bookbinding. When she moved to London, she decided to continue her bookbinding studies.

She now says that one of the reasons she took this direction was that she felt uprooted. "I found I didn't want to paint in London because I felt no contact with my surroundings — no contact with what was deep and emotional. Even today when I go home there's a change of gear, a sense of recognition."

Shannon's approach to bindings is in one sense a technical one. She remarks: "It's the invention of it that I like." Each book is treated as a separate problem, with its own very distinct parameters — format, subject and client. She states: "If any bindings of mine were to be set side by side I would hope they would not be recognized as being the work of one person — that each would be as different as people are from one another. Not for the sake of anonymity, but because every book is an entirely

Above: Faith Shannon's tools are as neatly ranged as the objects in her collection.

Right: Binder Trevor Jones examines some of the preparatory work for one of his complex designs.

different problem of purpose and structure, and therefore of materials and appearance."

As a result of this practical approach, she has built up a reputation as being perhaps the most original of living binders in her approach to materials. For example, she recently bound a copy of a botanical work, *The Genus Crocus* by George Maw, for the Hornby Library in Liverpool. The binding is a dark green Italian morocco, and the front board is modeled with papier maché and balsa wood, so that it takes the shape of an eye, with a convex plate-glass lens inserted to make the eye itself. Under the plate-glass, and protected by it, is a piece of vellum painted in watercolor. It shows the iris of the eye, and, growing from it, crocuses in several colors. Miss Shannon says that she meant to allude to the fact that crocuses are members of the genus iris. Another recent binding, this one for the *Times Atlas of the Moon,* is in black Oasis morocco, with, on each cover, a sunken central panel made of black suede. The moon, shining full on one panel, and crescent on the other, appears on both covers, and is inlaid in translucent mother-of-pearl.

Her total originality is perhaps one of the things that have prevented Miss Shannon from committing herself to binding full-time. By nature a solver of problems, she has extended her activity into the field of book illustration, and into designing containers. She is also currently working on commissions for the decoration of porcelain and ceramics. And she continues to paint. Because her other activities, and also because of the elaboration of some of her work,

"It's a nice exercise—one I've yet to succeed in — to try and design bad taste into a binding"

she only produces about nine bindings a year, so that her books are collector's pieces in more than one sense.

The fact that Shannon is the very contrary of prolific does, of course, distinguish her quite sharply from the binders who worked for the great bibliophiles of the past. These clad, not specimen volumes, but whole libraries. Yet at the same time, she clearly has close links with the world of traditional bookbinding. She is very insistent that the book should continue to work as a physical object: "It's no good doing it and then finding it doesn't open." It is significant that she was one of the expert binders who went to Florence to help repair the books which had been damaged in the great flood of 1967.

My third binder, Trevor Jones, is more willing than Miss Shannon is to accept the fact that a book which has passed through his hands is no longer primarily a reading copy. He is also the most insistent of the three binders on choosing the book for himself he is going to bind, rather than accepting a commission. He says: "The method of working I favor is one in which the design evolves as the binding progresses. I begin with a concept which is often only precise in the choice of materials, colors and methods of procedure – so the *form* of the design, especially in details, can be modified in the course of binding. It's what David Pye *(The Nature of Design)* calls the workmanship of risk – an adventure, the result of which can't be predicted. This is fine if I'm binding for myself. If it works, it is

exhibitable; if not, I can hide it or strip it down and start again."

It is perhaps this philosophy which has prevented Trevor Jones from making bookbinding the economic center of his activity. He is head of the Art Department at St. John's College, York, and carries a heavy teaching schedule.

He is perfectly conscious that much of what he has to say about his craft cuts across the traditional craft aesthetic. He asserts, "I think good taste bedevils bookbinding, and stands in the way of turning it into an art form. Using good material tastefully generally gets in the way of making art." He adds: "It's a nice exercise – one I've yet to succeed in – to try and design *bad* taste into a binding."

In a recent catalogue-note he writes,
The fact, that we spend such time and effort in producing useless objects – or rendering objects less useful through our efforts (I find I can never read a book once I have re-bound it) – leads me to believe that we are indeed creating art objects. The one infallible test of a work of art is its intrinsic uselessness. The making of art is magic and there must be something magical in fine binding for us to perpetuate an activity so out of key with the universal trend to systematization. I astonish myself by continuing the practise: it must be that I am a true amateur – I do it for love.
This radicalism is stressed by the kind of books that he elects to bind. Recent bindings include one for

154

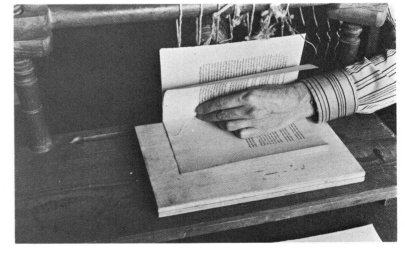

Trevor Jones using a
sewing-frame. However
avant-garde the designs, the
basic techniques of hand
bookbinding remain firmly
traditional.

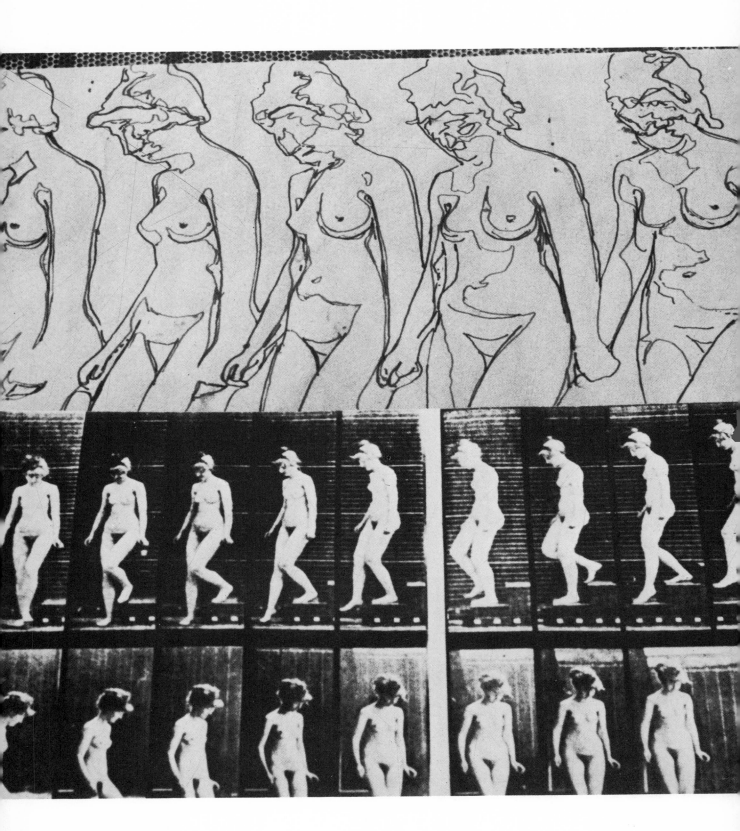

How Jones's designs evolve. For a book called The Amazons, he began with a Muybridge photograph, made a drawing, and then a stencil.

Joyce's *Ulysses,* one for the Marcel Duchamp/Richard Hamilton volume *The Bride Stripped Bare by her Bachelors Even;* and one for Ron Padgett's *The Adventures of Mr. & Mrs. Jim and Ron,* which has illustrations by the Pop artist Jim Dine. As a tribute to Dine's fascination with articles of clothing, the binding for this last incorporates an old gauntlet that Jones picked up on the seashore.

Jones does not deny that the technical aspects of binding continue to fascinate him — though he tends to denigrate his own powers as a technician. Nevertheless, as with more conventional craftsmen, one of the things which interest him is the need to invent ways of solving particular problems. He admits: "The problem-solving bit is an interesting aspect — not only in the craft, but outside it." And he speaks of the way in which a method invented to solve a particular difficulty — that is, prompted by the concept he may happen to have in his mind's eye — may then itself be modified to given a different effect when binding another book. In this second instance, the fact that the technique is already there, waiting to be used, has an effect on the form taken by the design.

In general, modern bookbinding seems to demonstrate with exceptional clarity the paradoxical nature of a great deal of contemporary craft activity. On the one hand, it has profound links with the ideas and standards of the past; and on the other hand it has been affected by the modernist philosophy which prevails in the fine arts. The result of the tension between the two poles, the two ways of thinking, has been an exceptionally powerful upsurge of creativity. It is doubtful, in fact, if bookbinding has ever been so imaginative and so brilliant in its effect as it is today. Certainly one would have to go back to the great bindings of the middle ages, with their jewels and carved ivory plaques, to find something which rivals modern work either in elaboration or in intensity of effect.

Laura Youngmark watches a
young visitor using a
table-loom.

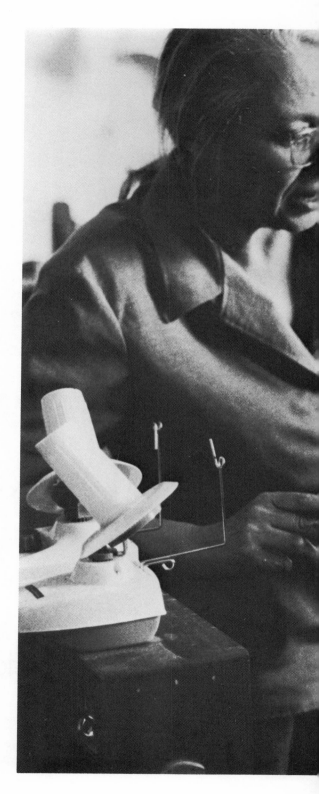

T he same mixture of the traditional and the
modernist that appears among bookbinders can also
be found in another group — that of the weavers.
Weaving is increasingly popular. Some craft
aficionados would feel that it now takes the same
rank as pottery, and for that reason will feel that I
have alloted too little space to it.

This comparative stinginess can be excused — or
at least accounted for — by two considerations. The
first is that there is a conflict of attitudes among
weavers between the traditional and the modern
which is so marked and so obvious that it can be
sketched in a very few portraits. The second is that
this is a book about professional craftsmen, and,
though there are many weavers today, weaving is,
par excellence, an amateur craft — an avocation
rather than a vocation.

Laura Youngmark and Nancy Childs are two
members of a group of four people — the others are
Rae Barnet and Mike Halsey — who recently set up
the Handweaver Studio and Gallery in North
London. The Gallery has several functions. It
operates as a center for the sale of handwoven and
allied textile, and there are also occasional
exhibitions. The studio attached to it can be used by
independent weavers, or people can take lessons
there. There is a well-stocked yarn store, and they
claim that they can also supply on request almost
any color and type of British fleece. When I visited
them, they were hoping to start a dyeing and wet
finishing area in the immediate future.

Recent though it is, the Handweavers Studio

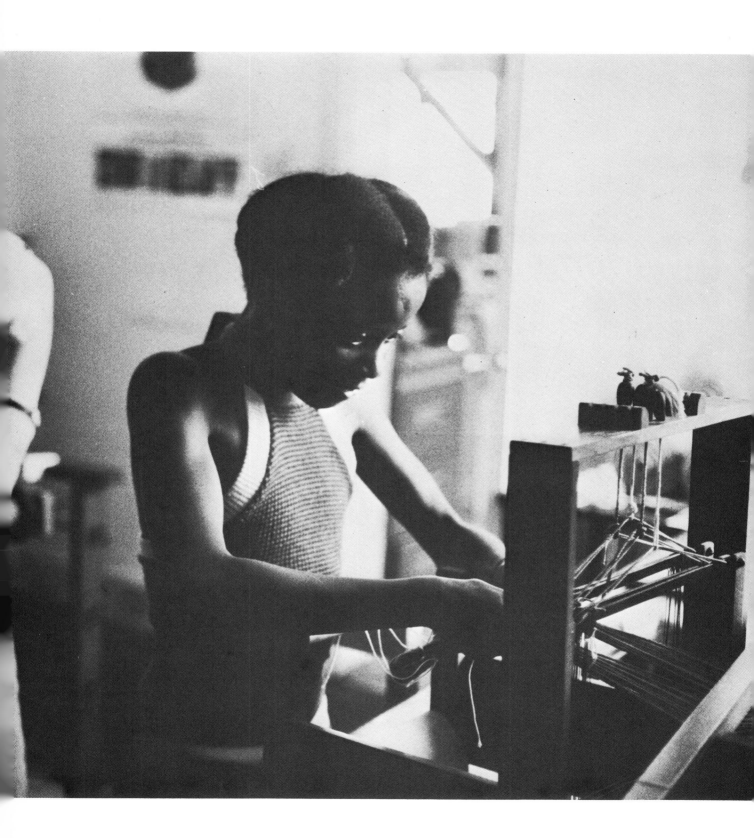

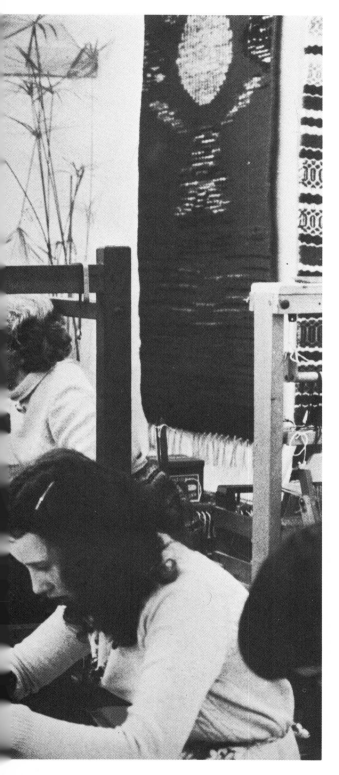

In the Cairnlee Weavery, Maria Halder gives advice to one of her students. In the foreground, less advanced pupils pick wool.

clearly stands at the center of a whole world of enthusiastic weavers and spinners. Both Mrs. Youngmark and Miss Childs are extremely active as adult education specialists. Both take the currently orthodox view of their craft, and the Handweavers Studio reflects their view by standing on the traditional wing of attitudes toward weaving.

This view has a strong ethical and moral element, best illustrated by quoting from the leaflet that describes the purpose of the enterprise with which they are connected: "The promotion of handweaving and allied textile crafts, as a means of achieving personal fulfillment and creative enjoyment based on sound craftsmanship and materials, will be the main aim of the Studio."

Laura Youngmark is exceptional among modern weavers in belonging to the fifth generation of a family professionally concerned with textiles. In her case, however, the concern did not manifest itself until comparatively late. She was born in Silesia, and came to England as a refugee in 1938. The profession she originally chose was catering, and she worked for a well-known chain of popular restaurants. Her conversion, or reconversion, to textiles, did not occur until after the war when, as she says, she "went for a walk past a loom-maker's shop." She is now extremely well known as a teacher.

Youngmark believes that the handloom weaver fulfils two objective functions, in addition to the subjective function of self-fulfilment and personal satisfaction. First, he or she can actually contribute

163

to industry. As she reminded me, the handloom is often the place to work out designs for mass production. The designer who works only with pencil and paper is unable fully to take into account the three-dimensional nature of the woven textile, where one thread crosses another. Using a handloom, he or she can search for the precise effect that is required, and can see how this must be achieved on the industrial loom.

For Mrs. Youngmark, nevertheless, the real point of handloom weaving is that it enables the craftsman to use techniques which are impossible for the weaver who works on a machine. As she points out, "a machine cannot change its mind every two minutes." As a creative weaver, the things that particularly interest her are the problems and opportunities offered by discontinuous wefts.

She passionately believes that weaving is a therapeutic and socially useful activity. She describes the immense increase in enthusiasm, and the drop in age, to be found among the people who come to her classes. She says: "Today it is secretaries and computer operators who take it up. When you live in the very midst of a modern society, you feel the need to use your hands; and the need, too, for the handmade article which has its own individuality, the character of one particular person built into it."

It was Mrs. Youngmark and Miss Childs who sent me to see the remarkable Maria Halder. Maria and her husband Johannes Halder form part of the community at a Rudolf Steiner home just outside Aberdeen, Scotland. The Rudolf Steiner homes, run on Christian and anthroposophical principles, look after severely disturbed and subnormal children. They attempt to deal with every type of mental abnormality, from severe neurosis (often accompanied by high intelligence) to Mongolism.

Like Mrs. Youngmark, Mrs. Halder was born in Germany. She and her husband did not emigrate to England until 1955. She had been a weaver since before the war — she began in 1936 — and had been working with mentally-handicapped children since 1952. "We found," she says, "that we couldn't work any more to make money, and found it more sensible to work in a community." She and her husband live entirely without wages, and anything they need comes directly from the community they live in.

Like many institutions, the Rudolf Steiner home at Bieldside has taken over what used to be a large private house. The building is full of institutional clatter. The children are friendly and extremely curious about strangers, but it doesn't take very long to become aware of the problems that have brought them here.

Mrs. Halder's weaving studio, a new addition recently designed by a young Scandinavian architect, stands beside the main block. The contrast between the house where the children live and the weavery is very striking. The restless, bustling atmosphere of the one is quite unlike the tranquillity of the other. A selected group of children come to work for two hours every afternoon, and the average

"When you live in the very midst of a modern society, you feel the need to use your hands; and the need, too, for the handmade article which has its own individuality, the character of one particular person built into it"

Maria Halder; a community life without wages.

The Cairnlee Weavery is a
purpose-designed building. All
looms are full size, but have
been adapted to have four
pedals only.

"Why, Maria — did I do that? That's a dress which is fit for a queen"

duration of their course in the workshop is around two years. Mrs. Halder says that she can look after as many as nine students at a time. She makes no reservation about those she takes, and is as willing to work with the severely subnormal as with the disturbed but highly intelligent (some of these latter, as she points out, can be violent and occasionally dangerous). She will not, however, keep on any child who, after a certain period, does not show signs of progress.

The reason Mrs. Halder teaches weaving is that the activity has a therapeutic effect: not merely is it calming in itself, but the physical movements involved are beneficial to children who have often lost all sense of bodily rhythm. "I won't use table looms," she says, "even though they might look simpler for beginners, because the rhythm is wrong. The big looms you see here use the whole body."

One rapidly learns that handloom weavers often have a certain puritanism about their equipment. There is a strong prejudice in favor of the wooden-framed, rather than the metal-framed loom, even though wood, which has a tendency to warp under stress, is much more difficult to keep "in tune" than the latter. Maria Halder probably belongs to this traditionalist school by instinct. The looms in her workshop, however, have all been modified in various ways to make sure that the children use them in the way she thinks best, just as the studio itself was built to her exact requirements. One notable feature of her studio is that the looms have only four pedals, rather than six. This modification

has been made in order to see to it that footpressure is applied evenly, with both feet being used at the same time.

To watch an afternoon's work at the Cairnlee Weavery is a moving experience. The children file in quietly and take their places in the large, tranquil, toplit room. The restlessness I have seen many of them display, when we lunched together in the dining room of the main block, seems to vanish immediately after they enter. There are few recurrences of it during the two hours we spend together — they work busily, while I take photographs of what they are doing.

Maria Halder creates the patterns for what is woven and then adjusts each pattern to the capacities of her pupils. They make rugs, and also fine silk, metal-thread and woolen material in lengths. These often incorporate elaborate color-changes based on formulae which are pinned to one of the uprights of the loom. Mrs. Halder believes that the satisfaction of making something beautiful is as therapeutic as the rhythm of the loom itself. She tells the story of a particularly fine length which, to please the girl who had woven it, she made into an evening-dress. The girl gave an exclamation of astonishment when she was shown the result: "Why, Maria — did I do that? That's a dress which is fit for a queen!"

Because the patterns make great demands on the children, and because of who they are, work proceeds slowly. Maria Halder hurries from one loom to another, sorting out whatever problem has

The young weavers derive great satisfaction from the weaving process itself, but this is undoubtedly validated by the knowledge that people want to have and use their products

arisen. No sooner has she solved a difficulty than a cry comes from another bench: "Maria! Maria! Please come here!" But there is always the feeling of a shared task, of working for a purpose. The two hours do not seem to last long.

It may be felt that what seems like a purely therapeutic enterprise has no place in a book of this type. One reason for describing it is that it demonstrates how handloom weaving can play an integral role within a special set of circumstances. Maria Halder does not believe in anything remotely approaching mass production – what will benefit the child is the only consideration – the products of the Cairnlee Weavery are widely distributed through the network provided by the Rudolf Steiner organization, which is international. Specimens of the children's work go as far afield as Switzerland and Norway. The young weavers derive great satisfaction from the weaving process itself, but this is undoubtedly validated by the knowledge that people want to have and use their products.

My two other subjects can both be classified as experimentalists. They are among the best known figures in their field of activity. One is Peter Collingwood. Collingwood, who was born in 1922, is a good example of the sudden change in pattern which a commitment to the crafts can impose. He first trained in medicine and qualified as a doctor in 1946. His interest in weaving was aroused when he was doing his Army service – at this time, he made himself a loom. He says the impulse was not at all romantic, but one of technical curiosity – how was it

that such a device could be made to produce a piece of cloth? "At first," he says, "I was far more fascinated by the process than I was by the product."

After training in several weaving studios, he set up his own workshop in London in 1952. "I decided I wanted to do rugs," he recalls, "and I argued everything back from time and cost. In order to make any sort of living, I found that I had to produce a rug every two days. So I had to experiment in order to find methods of making rugs in two days which looked different from other people's – for the market I was then operating in was remarkably narrow."

From this apparently unambitious start, Collingwood has gone on to make himself one of the best known of all British craftsmen. In 1963 he won a gold medal at the International Handicrafts Exhibition in Munich; in 1968 he published his book *The Techniques of Rug Weaving,* which has become a basic text for many weavers; and in 1969 he was the first living weaver to have an exhibition at the Victoria and Albert Museum in London. He shared this show with Hans Coper.

Collingwood now has a workshop in the former schoolhouse of the beautiful Suffolk village of Nayland. The place, he points out, was chosen not for its picturesqueness, but because it offered the kind of space he needed at a price he could afford to pay. In addition to making rugs, both flat and pile, he now also specializes in wall hangings to which he has given the generic title of "macrogauzes." These

Peter Collingwood at work making one of his 'macrogauzes.' The linen threads are bunched and tied to vary the pattern.

"All the designs I do arise out of the techniques I use . . . But I don't accept the loom itself as something 'given': I try to stretch the possibilities available to me by altering it in various ways"

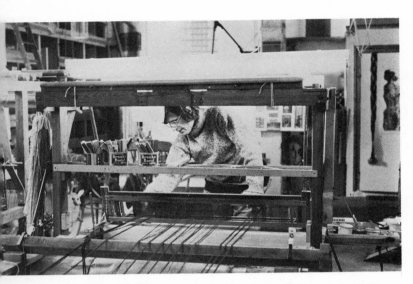

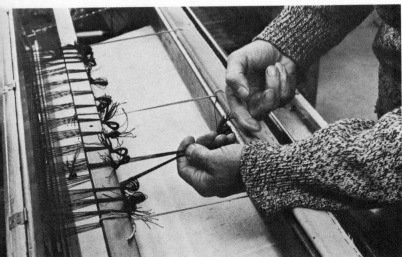

entail transposing groups of linen threads which are stabilized with fine steel rods. They often have a strongly three-dimensional effect. More solid-looking decorative pieces are produced by using an off-the-loom technique called "sprang." Collingwood has recently published a textbook on this latter method of weaving.

He says: "All the designs I do arise out of the techniques I use, just as they have done from the beginning. But I don't accept the loom itself as something 'given': I try to stretch the possibilities available to me by altering it in various ways. And often when you alter a loom for one specific purpose, you find that your alterations have unexpected side effects, which can lead you to the exploration of further possibilities."

He sees the work he does as being guided by certain limitations, both of technical possibility and of use. Freedom of weaving means slow production. The problem is to find a way of working which allows maximum flexibility of pattern within the period of time available. Symmetrical patterns, which are quicker to make, also have a logic of their own when used in creating objects such as rugs because, since a rug is made to be put on the floor, the pattern has to work from whatever angle it is approached. And the bilateral symmetry to be found in his macrogauzes has its roots in technique as well as in aesthetic preference — that is, it arises from the need to maintain even tension in the threads.

Though the macrogauzes, even more than the rugs, are entirely nonindustrial in nature,

Below, top: Winding wool. Collingwood usually works alone and does all jobs himself.

Below, bottom: A rug-loom specially adapted by Collingwood to produce complex patterns simply and quickly. The design is varied by moving the keys.

Collingwood feels no hostility to industry as such. As he points out: "I concentrate on the things that industry can't do." His current ambition is to be given the loan of a power loom for six months, so as to be able to work out precisely what its possibilities and limitations are, when related to his own extensive experience of the medium.

Ann Sutton is also interested in "pushing the possibilities of the medium as far as they will go." In her case, this has also meant an increasing interest in off-the-loom techniques. Ann Sutton is married to the furniture-maker, John Makepeace, whose work will be discussed in the next chapter. They live at Farnborough Barn, near Banbury in Oxfordshire, and she has a workshop of her own in a village about three miles away.

Miss Sutton has long experience as a teacher. She has also been a designer for industry. But equally important is her commitment to the fine arts. In 1967, she spent what she calls "a confirmatory period of work" with the sculptor Kenneth Martin. This encouraged her to think about textiles as being constructs, just like certain kinds of constructivist sculpture. "Every thread, and every kind of yarn," she says, "has its own nature. Some are soft and flexible, others are not. You have to discover the kind of construction, the way of locking the threads together, which best suits the material you are using. What you are looking for is not the complex solution, but the simple one. The way I've developed is to come out of complexity. I now try to pursue the simplest solution to any problem — and that, when

171

172

"I concentrate on the things that industry can't do"

you find it, often isn't at all the conventional one. In a way, this means that I'm a person who likes to do things as easily as possible – if you're a bit bone-idle, it helps!" And then again, she remarks: "I don't like traditional solutions to things if they are solutions which have been held on to until everyone has forgotten the reasons for them."

She feels that she is attracted to weaving by the fact that it imposes rules. She was born in North Staffordshire, and comes from a family which was connected with ceramics, but pottery has never attracted her: "The moment I touched clay I knew I didn't like it, because the medium was too docile."

"For me," she says, "it is the limitations of weaving that make it exciting. It really hurts to go on the wrong side of the road. At the same time, the rules I use have got to be very beautiful in themselves if they are to give me a buzz. I've got to feel that if I've applied the rules correctly then the resulting piece is going to look all right – even if I don't know beforehand precisely what the piece will be like. If you know, somehow it takes away the point of making it.

Today, she has reached the point where the rules she uses are often mathematical formulae. An idea for a new piece of weaving may express itself as a drawing, or it may equally well make its appearance as a set of numbers, moving across a series of columns according to a predetermined rhythm. "It's a bit ironical," she remarks, "if you know that one of the things I was hopeless at in school was mathematics."

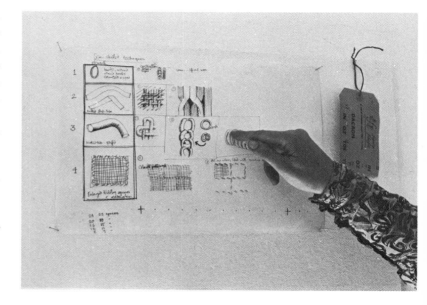

Opposite page: Ann Sutton broods about new possibilities in weaving.

Above: Some of Ann Sutton's work can be expressed in diagrams like this. But often she only needs a set of numbers to tell her what to do.

"I now try to pursue the simplest solution to any problem — and that, when you find it, often isn't at all the conventional one"

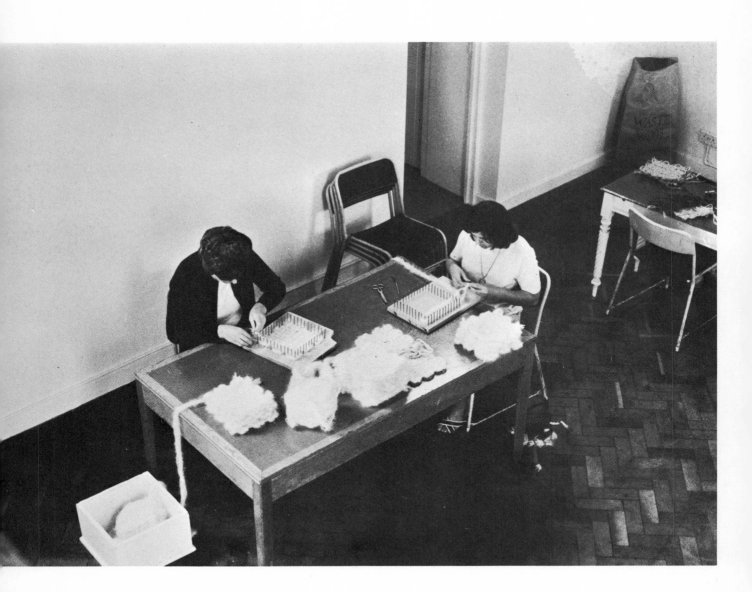

174

She is also endlessly inventive about how the fibers she employs are made into structures. A number of recent exhibition pieces have been made with the help of an old-fashioned stocking machine, of the kind used by outworkers for making hosiery during the earlier part of this century. A stocking machine of this type can be used to produce a knitted tube of almost any length, and this tube can be stuffed as it is made. Stuffed tubes of various colors, produced by this simple method, can be sewn and woven together to produce what are in fact soft sculptures, related to the work of Pop artists such as Claes Oldenburg. Ann Sutton comments: "I think that what these pieces demonstrate is the fact that I'm interested in structure — in basic, simple structure, and in the relationship between structure and materials. You make the piece because you want to see how the structure and the material click."

Her attitudes toward the idea of craftsmanship for its own sake might seem designed to upset most of her colleagues. "I can't see the reason," she says, "for fine craftsmanship by itself. What is wrong with faulty craftsmanship is that it detracts from the concept. I admire impersonal finish, and I like the idea that no human hand has touched a particular object. It's as if it were the inside of a banana. No human hand has touched that until you peel it."

Yet it is precisely this insistence on the logically constructed and thoroughly well-made which divides Ann Sutton from the work of avant-garde artists, whom she might otherwise seem to resemble very

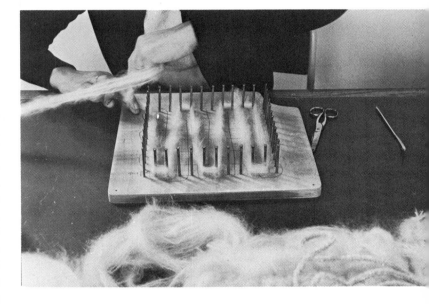

Opposite page: Village women at work in Ann Sutton's new workshop. None of them are trained weavers.

Above: The simple frame which Ann Sutton has devised for weaving woolen squares for bedspreads.

175

"Every thread, and every kind of yarn, has its own nature. Some are soft and flexible, others are not. You have to discover the kind of construction, the way of locking the threads together, which best suits the material you are using"

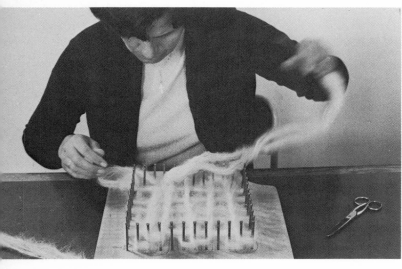

This sequence of pictures illustrates how the frame shown on page 175 is used. The frame consists of a wooden board with some long nails. The square is built up using a continuous thread.

closely. She criticizes the avant-gardists for their failure to follow their own announced rules and for the poor finish of many of the objects they produce.

Another thing which distinguishes Sutton from the avant-gardists is her continuing interest in the workshop situation. The weavery she has set up near her home is probably the most unusual to exist anywhere. She relies on part-time work by local women, none of whom have any training as weavers. She has invented off-the-loom techniques which give luxurious results, but which can be mastered in less than an afternoon. When I visited this workshop it was only in its third day of operation, but three women workers produced, with the aid of a simple frame, almost enough loosely woven squares to make a fair-sized bed cover. An experienced weaver would probably have needed the best part of three days to produce the same area of fabric on a loom. Ann Sutton sees no particular moral benefit in doing things the difficult way. Her hero is not William Morris or anyone like him, but Edward de Bono, the inventor of lateral thinking. "I was so thrilled to read his book," she comments. "It defined for me things I had been doing for years."

Laurence Whistler at work on
a bowl for the Philadelphia
Museum.

It often seems easier to gain an insight into the craftsman and his craft by concentrating not on what he makes but on the circumstances surrounding his activity. Does he work by himself, or with others? How much physical effort does his activity require? How much equipment does he need? Must he work in a place specially adapted to his needs, or can he set up shop almost anywhere?

After having looked at the majority of the craftsmen in this book according to what they produce, let us examine the remainder with an emphasis on the circumstances in which they work. The same substance can often respond to very different methods. For example, Mike Joslin and George Eliot work with glass; and so does Laurence Whistler. But this circumstance apart, there could scarcely be a greater contrast in what they do. Joslin and Eliot are glass blowers – a particularly athletic, even balletic form of craft activity. Whistler is a glass engraver. His occupation is probably the most solitary, and – dare one say it without too much impertinence? – the most introverted recorded in this book.

Glass engraving is peculiarly demanding, in that mistakes cannot be erased and are often difficult to cover up. But the rewards are commensurate with the rigors, because lead glass gives every line drawn upon it something of its own clarity and purity. Whistler understands its particular qualities. As he says in a recent book: "Glass is an ideal medium for expressing the ambiguous, having ambiguity in its very nature... Full of illusions itself, glass calls for

"Glass is an ideal medium for expressing the ambiguous, having ambiguity in its very nature"

"The Overflowing Landscape," a recent bowl by Laurence Whistler. Some of the engraving is on the inside and some on the outside of the glass.

an illusionistic art, and would do so even if this could be banned in all visual arts by the fiat of fashion."

Whistler began his career as a poet, a profession at which he now considers himself to have been a failure in spite of his having published numerous books of verse. His glass engraving began when, prompted by accounts of Queen Elizabeth I and courtiers writing poems in this way, he tried engraving verses with a diamond on a windowpane. He was later inspired by the Dutch diamond-point engravers on glass who flourished during the seventeenth century, and from this beginning has created an art form peculiar to himself, using lead crystal goblets and bowls as grounds upon which to draw.

The work of the craftsmen whom Whistler regards as his predecessors would usually have served some heraldic or commemorative purpose. Whistler's glasses and bowls have little to do with this kind of purpose. Each of his pieces is the equivalent of a poetic metaphor, or a series of interconnected metaphors. "My aim," he writes, "is to represent an actual scene, or more often an invented one, in such a way that it will seem to have significance, to make the looked at have the look of being meant — whether the particular meaning is clear, as in obvious allegory, or doubtful."

The tools he uses are simple — a diamond or steel point, and a portable electrically-powered revolving drill for broader effects and for filling in textures. These instruments need to be manipulated, of course, with extraordinary sureness and delicacy of

Photograph: Graham V. Herbert

touch. But they can, on the other hand, be used in almost any circumstances. All the craftsman needs is a good light which will let him see what he is doing. The work makes more demands on the nerves than on the physique, as it needs less pressure to make a mark with the diamond point than it does to make one with a pen.

Whistler's skill probably surpasses that of any of his predecessors, though he is reluctant to make the claim. His imagination is certainly much wider ranging than theirs. He has increasingly broken away from the conventions which governed, or seemed to govern, the use of his medium. Not for him the coats of arms and inscriptions which were the standard product of the seventeenth- and eighteenth-century engravers. One reason his technique is so refined is that the effects he imagines need new methods of expression. Though the technique retains its simplicity, he applies it in original ways.

In a recent bowl, entitled "The Overflowing Landscape", Whistler shows a bedroom with a framed landscape hanging on the wall. This landscape seems to stream out of its frame and to come round the side of the bowl again to invade the room that it initially burst out of. The details of the bedroom are engraved on the inside of the glass, but the truant landscape is on the outside, and therefore, as Whistler says, seems more remote, more dream-like than the rest.

The tranquil circumstances, and the minimal physical effort, which were required in order to create this masterpiece, are in striking contrast to the way Joslin and Eliot create their delicate, multicolored goblets, vases and lampshades in the Tiffany tradition.

A glass blower's workshop is necessarily an active place — the molten glass can be blown and otherwise worked upon for only a few moments at a time, and the whole process of handling it, at the end of long rods and blowpipes, develops a pronounced physical rhythm which has something extrovert and theatrical about it. The glassworks in Venice, and particularly in Murano, have always been a popular spectacle. Joslin and Eliot also work in public: their small rural museum often has a crowd of schoolchildren and other visitors in attendance.

In many ways, their mode of work corresponds to a stereotype which people have in their minds about the crafts. Many of us still half-believe that the craftsman, because he exercises his skill and his creativity on such an obviously physical level, is less sophisticated than we are.

Joslin and Eliot discredit the traditional notion about markedly physical forms of activity, which holds that those who turn to them are likely to be inarticulate. Like most modern craftsmen, they have clear ideas about what they do and why they do it. Mike Joslin is a very recent graduate of the Royal College of Art. At the age of 27 he has behind him, as he says, eight full years of being a student. George Eliot is more than ten years older. He, like a number of other craftsmen, started his career as a designer. It was only after working for some years in

At Bewdley Museum: looking through the window at the glass blowers' workshop.

Below: George Eliot begins to blow a glass vessel.

Above, right: Here the glass bubble has nearly reached the size he wants.

Below, right: Mike Joslin working on a piece of still molten glass.

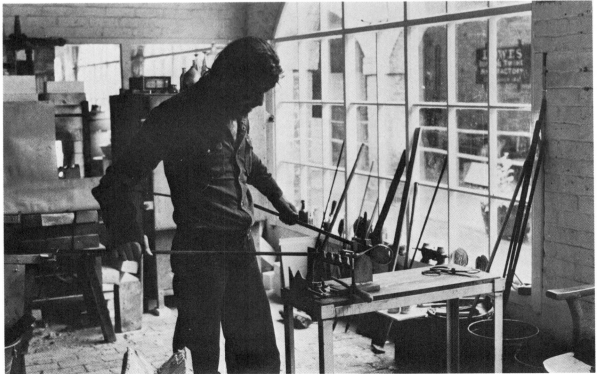

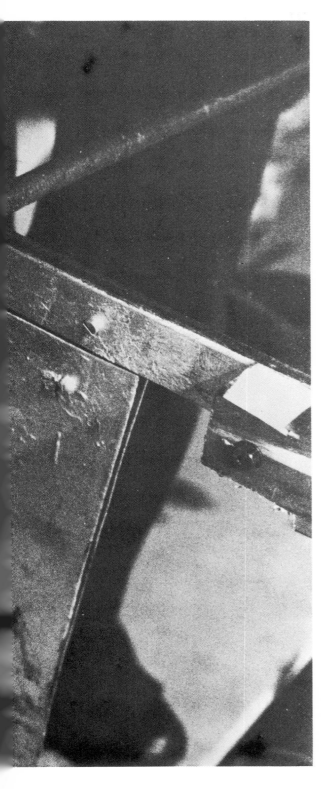

'Hooking,' one of the traditional methods of creating a decorative effect in colored glass.

the glass industry that he decided to make the stuff himself: as he says, "it was no good working at second hand."

Eliot's career is, in fact, a good example of the way in which the new craft tradition can sometimes have links with an older industrial one. He began his training at an art college in Stourbridge, which is the traditional center of the British glass industry. After graduating and working as a designer, he became increasingly fascinated with the skills that many of the older Stourbridge workmen still possessed — latticino, hooking, threading and so forth — even though, in modern conditions, they were seldom called upon to use them. He recalls that they, in turn, were somewhat puzzled by his interest: it never occurred to them that the dexterity they had acquired might easily be put to use outside the factory.

Being younger than Eliot, Mike Joslin has had less contact with a surviving tradition of virtuoso workmanship in glass. He has had to reinvent for himself techniques which were obviously well known to the workmen who produced glass for the great Art Nouveau designers such as Tiffany. He finds this disappearance of knowledge frustrating. He feels, too, that glass suffers from the comparison which is sometimes drawn between studio glass makers and the far more numerous studio potters. People, he thinks, look at glass as if it were clay, while the standards of judgment ought to be different. In addition to this, glassmaking has, he says, tended to become a kind of refuge for

Mike Joslin begins work on a
decorative glass lampshade.
The chair he is sitting in is a
traditional and very functional
piece of equipment.

Joslin views glassmaking as
a perpetual search for a
difficult kind of satisfaction—
the moment when skill,
intention and judgment are
perfectly matched

191

Here we see how the lampshade evolves. Joslin has to work quickly while the material is still soft and malleable. He takes the bubble he has blown, opens it out, and flares the opening with tongs. Eventually the shade is sprayed with metallic oxide to make it iridescent.

artist-craftsmen who are failed potters, since it seems like an easier and less demanding form of activity.

In fact, what attracts him to glass is its marvelous tractability; and that this tractability — which means that the material can be coaxed into almost any shape, and tinted any color — is also what he thinks of as its principal disadvantage. Failures in glassmaking are just as likely to be failures of taste as they are to be failures of skill. Joslin views glassmaking as a perpetual search for a difficult kind of satisfaction — the moment when skill, intention and judgment are perfectly matched. For him, the workshop situation he shares with Eliot is essentially an arena, in which both can try their skills, and can urge each other on to greater finesse in handling their materials.

The equal partnership of Joslin and Eliot is an example of one kind of workshop situation. Another, quite different kind is the situation where the workshop is dominated by the personality of one man, who has a number of assistants to help him. At their most ambitious and best-organized, such workshops are (so many people would think) on the very borderline of craft. The operations which take place in such a context come very close to being industrial production on a small scale.

A good instance of this kind of workshop organization occurs in the production of fine silver. Silverware of any quality, whether imaginative or unimaginative in design, does not call for assembly line conditions. Even so, there are few, if any, silversmiths who would forgo altogether the use of

192

machines. Machines can do particular jobs – polishing, for example – as well or better than the unaided hands. And few professional silversmiths find it possible to work without assistants. The more successful a craftsman in this field becomes, the more likely it is that he will reserve the design work for himself and leave most of the production work to others. This is clearly a pattern which was followed by the great silversmiths of the past – by Lamerie and Paul Storr, for example.

Michael Driver, who has a workshop in a fashionable part of London, could reasonably claim to be the direct and legitimate descendant of such classic silversmiths. He has a thorough training in the craft he practices, but as his business has expanded (managed by himself and by his wife Pennie) he spends less time at the workbench, and more of it in making designs which his young and enthusiastic staff will carry out. Of course there is a great deal of give and take in this situation, as he points out, since they all work so closely together. A new design idea usually begins with Driver. It originates as a sketch and then as a detailed drawing. Only later will he experiment with it in metal, and this step is, in any case, often omitted. When the drawing has been handed over to one of the senior craftsmen, the latter will start to make it up, but may well return to Driver with suggestions for altering a profile, or for a different approach to making the piece, in the light of workbench experience. Driver is thus in close contact with the physical process of making, but may not participate

Michael Driver, silversmith.
Much of his work is done at
the drawing board.

directly in it himself.

The fact that Driver has a salesroom on the ground floor of the premises he occupies also encourages direct contact with the customer. Some of the silver is produced for stock. These items will quite often be repetitions of designs which the workshop has made for some years. But Driver will, from time to time, find himself attracted to a particular design theme and will produce a new collection of different items, all of which embody his idea. These will be put on show in the shop for clients to see. Often, however, a client will ask for a piece which is in the same style, but which doesn't actually figure in the collection – a larger or smaller jug, a taller or squatter coffee pot. And from time to time he will, of course, make a piece which is commissioned for some special purpose. He says that he has learned the need to have something there for the potential client to look at. It may not be precisely what the client needs, but it gives him the "feel" of Driver's style in a way that a drawing cannot do.

Robert Welch occupies workshops which were once used by Ashbee and the Guild of Handicraft. His setup is one of the most practical, yet in some ways one of the most complex of all those that I visited. Welch is equally known as a silversmith and as an industrial designer.

The contrast between Ashbee's approach and Robert Welch's is in many ways very striking. As Alan Crawford says, in his introduction to a recent book on Welch's work:

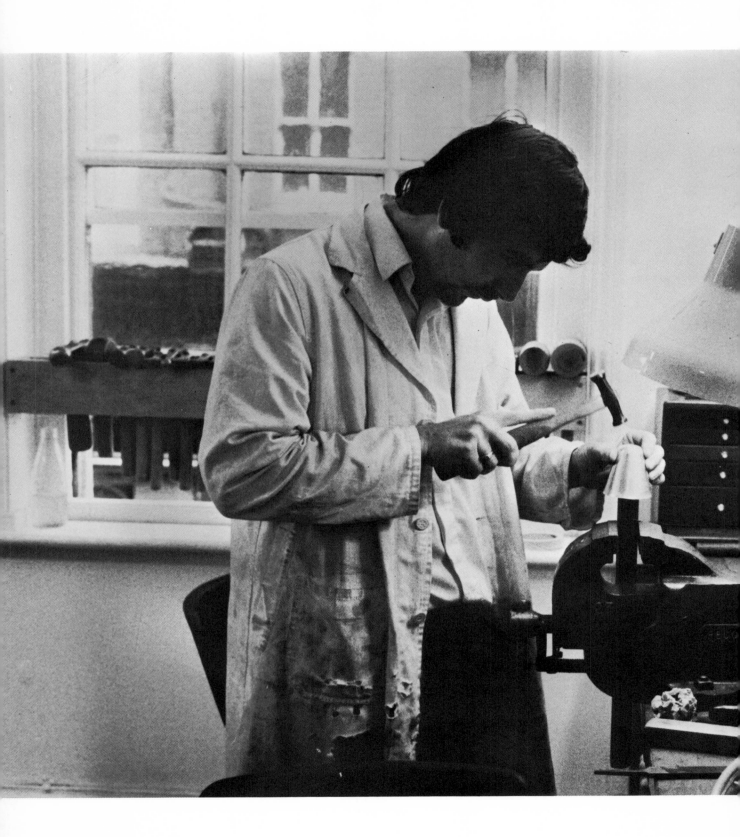

Chris, Michael Driver's principal assistant, forms a piece of hollow-ware in the workshop.

For Ashbee, Campden meant the atmosphere of a pre-industrial way of life, and, sadly, financial failure owing to poor communications, getting out of touch. For Robert Welch in the 1950's Campden meant, and still means, a congenial base for work that fits in various ways with industrial production, and happily, thanks to good communications, keeping in touch.

Welch was originally brought to the premises he now occupies not by a romantic desire to revive the Guild of Handicraft (about which he then knew little), but by the need to be near a firm which was producing his tableware designs in stainless steel. At the same time, he intended to build up his practice as a silversmith. In his mind, industrial work and work in the crafts go hand in hand and constantly fertilize one another. He admires the precision and high quality of finish which can be achieved by industrial methods, and thinks these are in harmony with the craftsman's basic aims. And, at the same time, he is keenly interested in effects which can only be achieved by borrowing or adapting industrial techniques. Ann Sutton's use of a stocking knitting machine in order to produce some of the most interesting of her recent pieces is paralleled by the way Welch employed an old swaging machine, originally designed to make watch parts, to make the pattern of spherical forms that decorates a magnificent silver candelabrum.

Since he first set up his workshop in 1955 Welch has been offered, or has made for himself, constantly

Robert Welch in the workshop
at Chipping Campden.

expanding opportunities as an industrial designer.
He has designed cast iron cooking wares, clocks,
lamps, sanitary fittings and crockery.

His method of work has always started from the
study of the techniques to be employed on a
particular job. Later come drawings, then models.
"We're very extravagant with models," he says.
"We get the shapes right before we turn them into
silver."

And he then adds: "I never *believe* a drawing
until I actually see it made up into a
three-dimensional object — even I can kid myself
when a thing appears in only two dimensions. But
the great danger with models is that you are
sometimes tempted to depart from the original
conception. The physical presence and reality of the
model somehow distort what you had in your mind's
eye."

To visit Welch's workshop is to become aware
of a logical, but in some ways deliberately distanced
relationship between the idea in the designer's mind
and the working process which embodies that idea in
its final form. This relationship is expressed through
the physical disposition of space. The young
silversmiths he employs have a space on the same
floor as Welch's own drawing office, but separated
from it by the room used by his secretary and by a
length of corridor. Welch says: "I feel no guilt or
regret about not doing much direct silversmithing
myself. In the old days, when I slept on a camp bed
in the workshop, of course I did it myself. But now I
have so many commitments, so many things I want

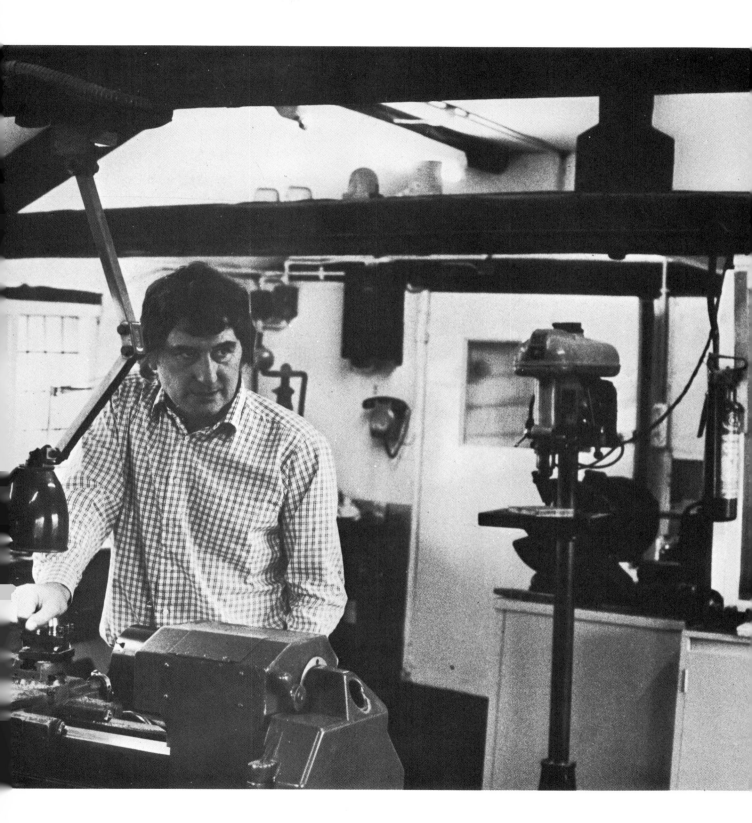

"I never believe a drawing until I actually see it made up into a three-dimensional object — even I can kid myself when a thing appears in only two dimensions"

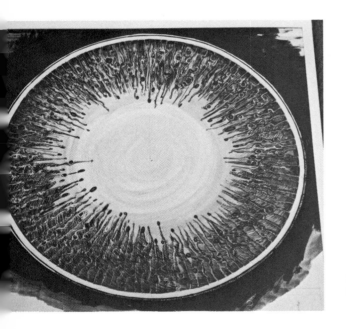

Opposite page: Robert Welch holds a spectacular dish designed by himself. The materials are silver, silver-gilt and numerous small amethysts.

Left: The original design for the dish shown on the opposite page.

Below: A visitor looks through the window of Robert Welch's shop in Chipping Campden. A full range of his silver is on view, and many other objects designed by him can be bought there too.

At Chipping Campden: one of Welch's designs is coming to birth under the skilful hands of one of his assistants.

to do, that I have to pace myself. If I worked at the bench, I'd no sooner get into the workshop than I'd be called away again. That would be frustrating for me and frustrating for my staff. The most useful contribution I can make is to do the thinking and make models which embody that thinking. I use the fellows in the workshop as extensions — that is their role. I often find it better to keep slightly away from them, so that when necessary I can look at what they are doing with fresh eyes."

Another aspect of Welch's multifaceted activity illustrates his close concern, not only with the form imparted to the objects he designs, but with the way they are used. In 1969 he bought a house a few yards from his workshop and turned it into a shop where his silver and other products are sold. He thus gets a direct feedback from the people who buy and use what he creates. New ideas happen as a direct result of what the shop customers ask for.

Welch's situation contrasts with that of Richard La Trobe-Bateman. It is not merely that Welch designs silver and La Trobe-Bateman makes furniture. It is that one is established, and the other is at the start of his career.

Perhaps because he is younger than Welch, La Trobe-Bateman is a clearer example of the kind of revolt which is increasingly common in the crafts — a revolt, not so much against the situation in industry as against the situation in the fine arts. Not that La Trobe-Bateman's experiences with industry have been especially happy. He trained as a sculptor, and during his time as a student wrote a thesis on "The

"I had the courage to do things badly"

Shape of the Car" (he belongs to the generation which felt the full impact of Pop Art). He then went to Detroit, ready to put his ideas into practice. He worked for a Ford subsidiary and learned the technique of industrial wax-clay modeling. Later, he worked for the British automobile industry but says flatly: "I wasn't good at it."

It was only after these varied experiences that he decided to train as a furniture maker. Even here, he notes, the training did not altogether suit the purpose he had in mind, as the course was directed toward teaching students how to *design* furniture, rather than how to make it. "There were always craftsmen around who could do it much better than you could," he remembers, "and you were supposed to let them carry out your ideas." When he set up an independent workshop, he found he had to retrain himself, and says he did it largely by reading two well-known handbooks for the amateur, Charles Hayward's *Tools for Woodwork* and *Light Machines for Woodwork*. He says that he found he had to develop "the courage to do things badly."

After this relatively slow start, he is not as yet wholly independent. His wife works, and he himself teaches sculpture at an art school for two days a week. At first, most of his commissions came from friends. Recently, as a result of exhibiting his work, they have started to come in from people he does not know. Yet he did not exhibit without some misgivings. He is not sure how far his own philosophy of work and workmanship fits in with anything officially approved. In the first place, he

Opposite page: Richard La Trobe-Bateman at work on a component for a piece of furniture.

Above: The chairs in Richard La Trobe-Bateman's dining room are all designed and made by him. No two are exactly the same.

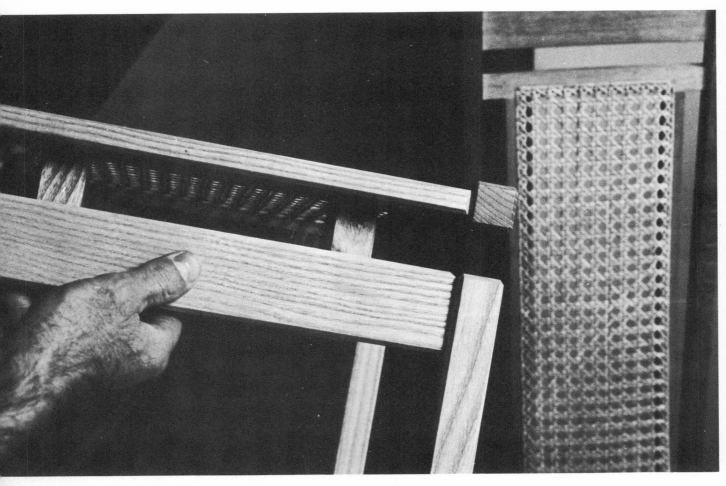

Above: Expressive workmanship. La Trobe-Bateman likes the method of construction to show.

Opposite page, above: La Trobe-Bateman is another craftsman who keeps elaborate notebooks.

Opposite page, below: La Trobe-Bateman in his living room. In the foreground is a constructional toy he made in his spare moments.

"I might suddenly make a chair that is hopeless and impractical, but so beautiful — would that be furniture or would it be sculpture?"

finds himself wanting to work increasingly freely, to "show the toolmarks and break down the mechanical finish." And in the second place, he is not quite sure what he feels about the supposed primacy of function. "I might suddenly make a chair that is hopeless and impractical," he remarks musingly, "but so beautiful — would that be furniture or would it be sculpture?"

John Makepeace, the best-established furniture-maker in England, illustrates the path of development La Trobe-Bateman might possibly follow, though it is by no means certain that he will.

Makepeace set up his own studio nearly fifteen years ago, and moved to the premises he now occupies in 1963. His workshops are next door to the house he lives in, and the complex — basically a group of converted and rebuilt farm buildings — also includes a small showroom. He is married to the weaver Ann Sutton, but she now has her own workshops a few miles away ("otherwise I'd never get anything done"). From eight in the morning onwards, Farnborough Barn is a hive of activity.

Makepeace's pattern of work resembles Robert Welch's in general outline but differs in many details, which are dictated not only by the difference in what they make but by differences in temperament. Thus, though Makepeace, like Welch, is the fountainhead from whom all the creative ideas flow, he participates actively in the physical work required. "For me," he says, "it's important to keep the making and the design in balance." He may begin the day by visiting each workshop in turn —

Below, top: Farnborough Barn, where John Makepeace lives and works.

Below, bottom: Inside one of the main workshops at Farnborough Barn.

Opposite page: John Makepeace with Aran the Irish wolf hound. The dog is named after the famous cream-colored Irish sweaters.

upholstery, turning, cabinetmaking — giving assignments and discussing any technical problems which may arise. At this time he may also have a discussion with the professional draughtsman whom he employs to work up his rough sketches into finished blueprints — "I do a lot of my designing in odd moments on the backs of envelopes" — but after this he will settle down to working on one particular job.

The job may either be a commission or an experimental piece which is intended to explore some particular problem. Makepeace's work is widely admired for the daring of his designs, and also for the luxury of the materials and finishes. But the starting point is always people. "I'm fascinated with behavior," he says. "With why people do the things they do."

The commissions he receives can be of several different kinds. There is the large-scale quasi-architectural commission, which involves fitting out the interior of a whole building, or at least of a room or series of rooms, often within the limitations of a strict budget. He finds these projects fascinating despite the restrictions, as he is highly critical of architects: "I find they study the building, but not the people in it." He would like to concentrate more in work of this type, "so that one could make the house a direct extension of the person who lives in it and the way they live."

Related to work of this quasi-architectural kind are the jobs he does for people who have a specialized problem which only a purpose-designed

"I also think you've actually got to like the individual you're dealing with ... You've got to find out how a given piece of furniture will function in his life, and design it for that"

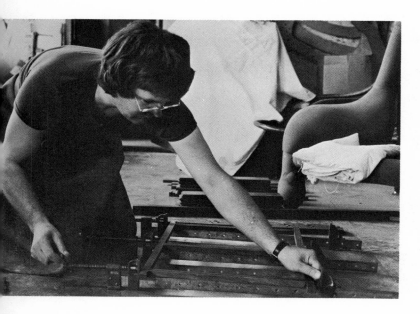

piece of furniture can solve. Makepeace has a high reputation as a maker of desks, and he recently created a desk for a translator of scientific papers. The problem was to enable the work to be done as quickly and with as little physical fatigue as possible. The client wanted, not to earn more money, but to have more leisure, and to be in a condition to enjoy it. Makepeace therefore studied his work pattern, noted what reference books he needed and where it was most convenient to have them. He noted, too, the fact that both original and translation were always on a standard paper size, and invented a structure which fulfilled all these needs and several others in addition (such as giving his client a view out of an awkwardly-placed window). The solution to the problem did not resemble a conventional desk at all but nevertheless worked efficiently.

Thirdly, there are commissions with a strong element of prestige and luxury, furniture made of fine woods, ivory, steel, lacquer, hide and acrylic. But these, however extravagant they may seem, are also answers to functional problems. When I suggested to Makepeace that this side of his activity had some resemblance to the service provided by a high-class tailor, he willingly accepted the comparison: "I hope I'm never as conventional as the big-name tailors, but you do want something which is suitable, does the job, and fits. I also think you've actually got to like the individual you're dealing with. He may have something in his mind's eye which isn't right for the way he is going to use it. You've got to find out how a given piece of furniture

Opposite page: Makepeace at work on the frame for a chest of drawers commissioned by the Philadelphia Museum.

Left, above: Makepeace talks to one of his apprentices. He starts them off on the simpler jobs.

Center: Makepeace himself is not happy unless he keeps in touch with the realities of hand workmanship.

Below: He is an extremely rapid worker. The job grows swiftly toward completion as one watches.

"In this age of speed and mass production, we are trying to slow things up a bit"

Robin Amis. Behind him is a spectacular carpet designed by Kaffe Fasset and made by the Weatherall Workshops.

will function in his life, and design it for that."

Finally, there are experimental pieces. Makepeace often uses these as a way of providing answers to questions which have arisen in his mind. Showing me a piece of furniture still in progress, he said: "Though it doesn't look like it now, this will be a small chest of drawers. I asked myself what a chest of draws actually *was*, and came up with the answer that it was a set of trays sliding in a frame. I then asked myself if the frame had to be the quadrangular thing you always see, and came up with the answer that it didn't. In this case, the trays will slide within a T-sectioned structure, which is what you see here."

All of these activities – the commissions and the occasional experiments – are regulated by careful attention to matters such as cost of materials, cost per hour and delivery dates. These are things which Makepeace has long accepted as part of the discipline necessary for survival in the field of activity he has chosen.

A contrast undoubtedly exists between the disciplined, centralized pattern perfected for themselves by Makepeace and Welch and what Robin Amis and his wife Lillian Delevoryas are trying to achieve at the Weatherall Workshops.

Far more deliberately than the other workshop situations I have described in this chapter, the Weatherall Workshops are meant to provide a measure of community spirit and a basis for a new way of living. Lillian Delevoryas says: "In this age of speed and mass production, we are trying to slow things up a bit."

Their workshop contrasts with that of John Makepeace, for example, because of the diversity of their present and planned activities. The workshop is based in a big old house in Gloucestershire. At the moment, the staple product is needlework, and designs for needlework. But there is a turner's workshop, which Robin Amis uses, and there are plans for other enterprises, such as designing tiles.

There is a close link between amateur and professional activity within the Weatherall context. During the week, it is the professionals who work in the house, but even these have not been professional for very long. Of the two embroideresses stitching away in the big livingroom, neither has trained as such. Sarah is a university student who stayed the full length of the course but didn't take her degree. She has come here, she remarks punningly, "by degrees." She admits that sewing is something she always hated before. Monica, who is Swedish, was until quite recently a nurse.

At weekends, the workshops are joined by numerous enthusiastic amateurs, who come partly in order to learn something more about needlework, and partly simply to share the pleasure of working with others.

The artistic inspiration for the enterprise is provided by Lillian Delevoryas herself. She is a Greek-American who trained as a painter. She says she started working with material seven years ago. She and her friend and colleague Kaffe Fasset have begun a revolution in needlework design which reaches well beyond the Weatherall context. The

212

Below: Monica at work on an ambitious piece of embroidery.

Opposite page: In her attic workroom, Lillian Delevoryas works on an appliqué-work hanging designed by herself.

"We don't pretend that everyone would be temperamentally suited to the kind of situation we want to make for ourselves. It does need a certain kind of dedication"

hidden part of her activity is the design work she does on canvases for amateurs, which are sold in leading needlecraft shops.

She says: "What we want to achieve here is a natural progression in work, which reaches out into the local community. In addition to our schools at weekends, the girls teach people who live nearby, who come for lessons on Monday nights. And they have a lot of freedom of decision in the big jobs you see, even though Kaffe or I may have provided the basic design. They take a lot of responsibility in matters like ordering and selecting wools. But we don't pretend that everyone would be temperamentally suited to the kind of situation we want to make for ourselves. It does need a certain kind of dedication."

As yet the Weatherall Workshops have only been going for just over a year and a half. During that time their brilliantly imaginative needlework and embroidery have won them a considerable reputation, and represent something quite new in a rather traditional field. What is fascinating about them in the context of the contemporary crafts, however, is the fact that they seem to represent a return to the very origins of the Arts and Crafts Movement. The ambition is not only to produce something beautiful, but to try and create a satisfactory framework for living, a framework within which the individual can realize his true potentialities and free himself from the pressures imposed upon him by modern society. The enterprise is trying to face precisely the same problems that confronted Morris and Ashbee. They are as essentially intractable and also as urgent. One is depressed by the fact that the situation has changed so little, yet filled with admiration for human persistence and optimism in continuing to confront it.

One of the difficulties in assessing the worth of the contemporary crafts, and the place they occupy in society, is that there is no agreed yardstick for measuring achievement. The reactions of the craftsmen and of those who come in contact with their products reveal a whole spectrum of judgments, many of them based simply on instinct or prejudice.

Let me try to give some examples which will illustrate this generalization. As we have seen from many of the interviews recorded here, the concept of virtuosity has survived in the crafts to a considerable extent, although it is now beginning to be questioned – see, for instance, what the bookbinder Trevor Jones has to say on this subject. Nevertheless, one of the pleasures that the finest craft products have to offer us is the feeling of astonishment at man's mastery over intractable materials.

At the same time, there is a strong feeling, inherited from the nineteenth century, and from the Arts and Crafts Movement in particular, that craft activity has a moral value, that the craftsman's way of life provides an example to others and offers a rebuke to those whose moral standards are less rigorous than his own.

There is a certain element of conflict in these two leading ideas. Can virtuosity, as such, coexist with the desire for total "honesty" of workmanship – for methods of making which clearly demonstrate the process of fabrication in the end result? Yet honesty of workmanship, interpreted in this rather narrow sense, is often held to be the validation of the craftsman's way of life and of his special position in society. The craftsman may thus be made to feel that he can only fulfil society's expectations by holding himself below his own true level of skill.

Another conflict arises over economics, and here the blame is often less the craftsman's than the customer's. When craft exhibitions are reported in the popular press, there is often a resistance to the level of prices charged. It is as if many people – and especially those who lack real experience of the crafts – automatically assume that the handmade product will be cheaper than the machine-made one. The craftsman is somehow expected to pass on his "integrity" and his "honesty" (or, to put it another way, his indifference to material gain) by not charging an economic price for his labor. No such expectation exists in the field of the fine arts. The artist, or his dealer, will charge what the traffic will bear. And an artist's reputation often rises in direct proportion to the prices he can get.

From my own observation, many professional craftsmen seriously undercharge for their work. They do so partly out of a feeling that the price they ask is already as much as the traffic will bear, but also because they think it wrong to squeeze the last penny out of work they enjoy doing so much. One would discover, if one examined the accounts of many craftsmen, that practically everything they make from their work is plowed back into their workshops, in the form of either tools or materials, and that in fact they rely on some outside activity such as teaching to provide them with the basic necessities of life.

Other craftsmen are simply content to live very near the poverty line, and indeed seem to feel that the film-star type of success which is sometimes accorded to fine artists would face them with problems they are not psychologically equipped to handle. Some seem to feel that, by accepting a low level of income, they identify themselves with the working class, or at least with the mythical worker who is the radical ideal.

As sociologists have long pointed out, level of income is no longer a safe guide in assessing whether a particular individual belongs to a particular class. As I said earlier, one of the most striking things about many artist-craftsmen is that their attitudes are middle-class. What they read, what they talk about, even their sense of humor, brings them closer to the salaried professionals in a bank than to the laborers on a building site. Most are highly educated, and most have a broad spectrum of outside interest. There are some, such as Robin Amis of the Weatherall Workshops, who have rebelled against some typically middle-class profession — in his case, that of advertising copywriter. But the majority, and certainly most of the younger ones, have a long professional training behind them in their own specialty. This training is on a level with that we give to lawyers or doctors.

One of the consequences of the original Arts and Crafts Movement was a change in the system of art instruction. Walter Crane, the Art Nouveau book-illustrator who was also a major force in art education at the turn of the nineteenth century, defined it as a switch from the "Academic or absolute" method of instruction to one he called the "Experimental or relative." Instead of being faced with a series of cut-and-dried procedures, the student was encouraged to experiment with materials and their properties. He was also taught to think in broadly visual terms, not necessarily within the orthodox limits of painting and sculpture. What this meant in practice was that craft skills began to be taught in art schools, under the heading of "design." The aim was not necessarily to teach the student to be a craftsman, but to open his eyes to the problems involved in making objects for everyday use.

In addition to educating fine artists, art schools therefore acquired the role of producing designers for industry. Many practicing craftsmen originally trained with the notion of making design their profession. But they belong to a generation which has renewed and sharpened the criticisms of industrialism and technology which were originally voiced by the more idealistic of the Victorians. This has led them to leave the industrial situation, and to try and find a way of living more in harmony with their own psychological needs.

If this harks back in the broad sense to Ruskin, one also finds very notable differences between the craft revival of the present day and the situation which existed before the First World War. The fine arts have passed through the violent and traumatic experience of Modernism, and the craftsmen have found it impossible to ignore the impact of the modernist Pioneers, ranging from Picasso to Andy Warhol, who have made so profound an impression on our way of looking at the world.

In many ways, Modernism may seem inimical to everything that the artist-craftsman stands for. An important element in the creative explosion which took place in the first decade of the twentieth century was impatience with the things that men like Morris, Ruskin, and Ashbee stood for. To the Futurists, with their worship of the machine, the craft revival seemed not only impossibly nostalgic but inextricably connected with the Symbolists, and it was Symbolism above all that they were determined to destroy. Even after Futurism had run its course, the machine retained its preeminence. The creators of the International Style in architecture, for instance, were in love with machine-finish, or at least with the semblance of it, to the point where they preferred to see it applied even to objects which were basically handmade. The only place where this stylistic dilemma was satisfactorily resolved was Scandinavia, which accounts for the leadership exercised by Scandinavian designers from the mid-thirties until at least the mid-fifties.

Even in the years after the Second World War, when Modernism was undergoing many changes, typified by the rapid succession of styles ranging from Abstract Expressionism to Pop Art, the climate of opinion did not seem favorable to the crafts. Craft activity seemed quaint and quixotic, without any real contemporary relevance. The painters' course of development led them from the extreme introversion of Abstract Expressionism to the detached irony of Pop Art, and finally to the strange and alarming numbness which characterizes Super Realism.

There are, of course, various turns and eddies in this stream of aesthetic events — they range from Dubuffet's fascination with the "wrong" or awkward way of doing things to Andy Warhol's wish to turn himself into a machine. But these quirks do not alter the basic impression one receives, which is not only that of the social and spiritual isolation of the artist, but of the ineloquence which he has deliberately imposed upon himself. However caught up he may be personally in the great issues and causes of the day, his art does not supply him with a means to comment upon them effectively. When contemporary artists band together to make a political point, what happens is one of two things. Either they commit only their voices, their energy and (should they happen to possess it) their prestige; or else they produce art of a purely occasional character, inferior to what they usually do, against the grain of their real preoccupations, and not only compromised but condescending.

One might suppose that the craftsman, the maker of objects, suffers from the same inability to make his opinions about the state of the world expressive in what he actually creates. It is true that recent attempts at "radical craftsmanship" have often seemed absurd. Political ceramics are rather worse, in aesthetic terms, than political pictures. There is also the inescapable fact that the craftsman is nearly always a producer of luxury goods, of things which only the more prosperous members of the community can afford. This is another reason that the craftsman tends to make a fool of himself if he goes in for politically extreme gestures.

Yet there is a real sense in which the craftsman is actually more in tune with society, and more aware of its needs, than the fine artist. On a purely practical level, craft work is often collaborative. The workshop situation provides its own social disciplines. In addition to this, many craft products are governed by the discipline of use. Chairs are made to be sat on, rugs are to be walked over, we take the casserole down from its shelf in order to cook a stew. By creating things like these, the craftsman is necessarily in touch with the people around him; and the forms he chooses inevitably say something about how he thinks they ought to live.

The crafts also benefit from what we may call good vertical communications. The craftsman is in touch with his contemporaries through what he makes, and with his predecessors and potential successors through the means whereby he makes it. The crafts, however inventive individual practitioners may be, still have a continuity of technique which is fast disappearing from the fine arts. There, objective knowledge of how to produce a particular effect has almost vanished — so much so that it is difficult for art schools to devise a sensible system of instruction.

Today the fine artist must discover not only his own themes but his own methods of embodiment, and even his own range of materials. This means that the link between an older and a younger generation of practitioners is weakened, for, in the most literal sense, they have little to tell one another. In the crafts this is not so. It is perfectly possible for a potter to learn from another potter's methods while totally rejecting his aesthetic.

Ease of communication on technical matters is probably the reason that the relationship between the professional and the amateur in the crafts is both easier and more productive than the relationship between the professional and the amateur artist. The relationship between the professional and the amateur is of major importance because it is increasingly likely to affect the way in which the arts are supported.

Support for the crafts, as well as for the fine arts, is likely to come increasingly from the public sector. It has for some years been accepted that the state, or other public bodies, should support the arts — that this is part of their complex duty toward society as a whole. This has led to the setting up, on both sides of the Atlantic, of innumerable official and quasi-official organizations. Each nation proceeds in this field very much according to its own traditions. Thus, we find a tradition of lavish municipal support for the arts in West Germany and the Netherlands, an inclination toward strongly centralized cultural institutions in France, a tendency toward keeping the arts at one remove from the organs of government in England and, in America, a feeling that much of the necessary finance should come from privately endowed foundations. But however different the mechanisms, the basic assumption is the same. Everyone in a democracy has the right to enjoy art. This principle sounds convincing until one realizes the degree to which it divides the artist from his audience. The professional produces art, the non-professional consumes it.

This situation increasingly dissatisfies the more committed sector of the arts audience. They would say that everyone in a democracy has the right to make art — and ought to be offered the facilities to do so. The craftsman is far better equipped to meet this demand than almost anyone connected with the fine arts because he does not have to revise his philosophy or even consider its implications.

To the modern fine artist, however ill-defined the boundaries of his activity have in practice become, Modernism is a state of mind. You either commit yourself completely, or you can make no claim to be an artist in any meaningful sense of the word. It is the simplicity of some of the gestures and techniques, and not their complexity, that makes this rigid frontier necessary. Thus, to choose a possible example, a contemporary sculptor may choose to express himself by creating small displacements within a landscape. He may, like the young English artist Richard Long, build a cairn of stones in a particular spot, and then document the act by taking a photograph.

But one can imagine a suburban ladies' art club — thirty or more middle-aged women — embarking on a bus for a weekend outing, in order to go and do just this in some suitable stretch of country. Does the mere fact of multiplication make their activity ridiculous, while the single pioneering gesture is undoubtedly serious? It is difficult to say.

Suppose only one of those suburban ladies built a cairn and photographed it, and then got back in her car and returned to her husband, her children, her golf, and her bridge playing? Does her action become "art," and if so, how? Does the art content depend on how the photograph itself is used? The maker may show it to her friends. Or she may enter it for a local photographic competition. Or she may get it exhibited at an avant-garde art gallery. It remains the same photograph — as simple to take as the cairn was to build in the first place. Nor is there any way of measuring a shift of content.

The situation in the crafts is different not only because the amateur and the professional aspire toward the same standard of skill, but because the skill itself, to some extent at least, is measurable. Though the question of personal taste remains, there is at least the assumption that, where technique is concerned, the good can be separated from the bad, and the better from the good.

Indeed, in some kinds of craft activity, the matter of professionalism versus amateurism has scarcely any importance. Embroidery, for instance, is so much the province of the enthusiastic amateur that we never pause to ask whether a particularly spectacular piece was done for love or done for a livelihood. The question is irrelevant to our appreciation of what has been accomplished.

This is one reason, I think, that amateur craftsmen seem to gain much greater satisfaction from what they do than amateur artists. They know they are playing in the same league as those who are labeled professionals. Few of us are humble enough to engage in creative activity without dreaming that we might one day rival the best practitioners in the field.

Yet, if the craft revival we are now witnessing can, in part at least, be attributed to a shift in attitudes toward "professional" creativity, there is one difference between the amateur and the professional craftsman which does emerge with unexpected force from many of the interviews which form the bulk of this book. This is that the best professional craftsmen, the most truly committed, are just as interested in process, in a dialogue with techniques, as they are in the finished object. The accomplished amateur craftsman often seems to take technique as something given, a rigid set of rules whose demands must be fulfilled. The inspired professional, on the other hand, alters the rules as he goes along and is always ready to exploit the unexpected consequences of any deviation from a set formula.

I believe that many of these questions about crafts and craftsmen are closely bound up with our hopes for humanity itself and our aspirations for the future. I find myself returning with renewed emphasis to the creativeness of the contemporary craftsman. His technical expertise may be impressive, but his inventiveness is still more so. His finesse in the use of materials is matched by a determination to make those materials speak in a new way. He refuses to produce objects in routine fashion, but tries to make each pot, each piece of weaving, each jewel, each bookbinding a fresh statement of possibilities. As a result, the possibilities themselves are constantly expanding. We see things being done in the crafts which seem to surpass anything previous generations could do. It is not surprising, therefore, that the crafts are attracting a new enthusiasm and attention from the public, or that their audience grows continually larger. The crafts used to be regarded as a last bastion against change, a means of preserving what would otherwise be lost and forgotten. Now the situation is quite different. The crafts are one of the few areas of human activity which continue to support the myth of progress, and the more dangerous but even more alluring myth of human perfectibility. Our descendants may wonder just as genuinely at the things we were capable of making in this age as we now wonder at the achievements of Chinese potters or Renaissance goldsmiths.